100 Hikes in™
THE ALPS

Second Edition

100 Hikes in™
THE ALPS

Second Edition

Vicky Spring & Harvey Edwards

THE
MOUNTAINEERS

I dedicate the French, Italian, and Swiss sections of this second edition to my wife Suzy Edwards, without whose tireless help and cooperation they would never have been written, and rewritten.

Harvey Edwards

© 1979, 1982, 1985, 1992 by Vicky Spring and Harvey Edwards

5 4
5 4 3 2

Published by The Mountaineers
1011 SW Klickitat Way, Seattle, Washington 98134

Published simultaneously in Canada by Douglas & McIntyre, Ltd., 1615 Venables Street, Vancouver, B.C. V5L 2H1

Published simultaneously in Great Britain by Cordee, 3a DeMontfort Street, Leicester, England, LE1 7HD

Manufactured in the United States of America

Copyedited by Kris Fulsaas
Maps by Karl Johansen and Helen Sherman
Cover design by Watson Graphics. Book layout by Erica Meyer
Cover photo: Hiker in Chamonix Valley, Mont Blanc massif in background. Photo by Kirkendall/Spring
Frontispiece: The Matterhorn and the hamlet of Findeln (Hike 33)
All photos by Kirkendall/Spring and Bob and Ira Spring unless otherwise noted

Library of Congress Cataloging in Publication Data

Spring, Vicky, 1953–
    100 hikes in the Alps / Vicky Spring & Harvey Edwards. —2nd ed.
        p.   cm.
    Rev. ed. of: 100 hikes in the Alps / Ira Spring. c1979.
    Includes index.
    ISBN 0-89886-333-3
    1. Hiking—Alps—Guidebooks. 2. Alps—Guidebooks. I. Edwards, Harvey. II. Spring, Ira. 100 hikes in the Alps. III. Title.
    IV. Title: One hundred hikes in the Alps.
GV199.44.A4S68   1992
914.94'7—dc20   92-18752
                                                            CIP

CONTENTS

Introduction   9

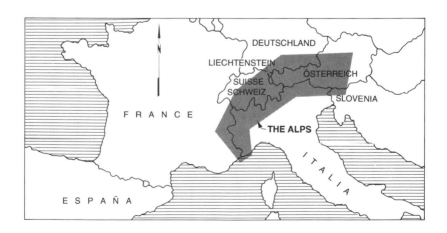

A Note About Safety

Safety is an important concern in all outdoor activities. No guidebook can alert you to every hazard or anticipate the limitations of every reader. Therefore, the descriptions of roads, trails, routes, and natural features in this book are not representations that a particular place or excursion will be safe for your party. When you follow any of the routes described in this book, you assume responsibility for your own safety. Under normal conditions, such excursions require the usual attention to traffic, road and trail conditions, weather, terrain, the capabilities of your party, and other factors. Keeping informed on current conditions and exercising common sense are the keys to a safe, enjoyable outing.

Political conditions may add to the risks of travel in Europe in ways that this book cannot predict. When you travel, you assume this risk and should keep informed of political developments that may make safe travel difficult or impossible.

The Mountaineers

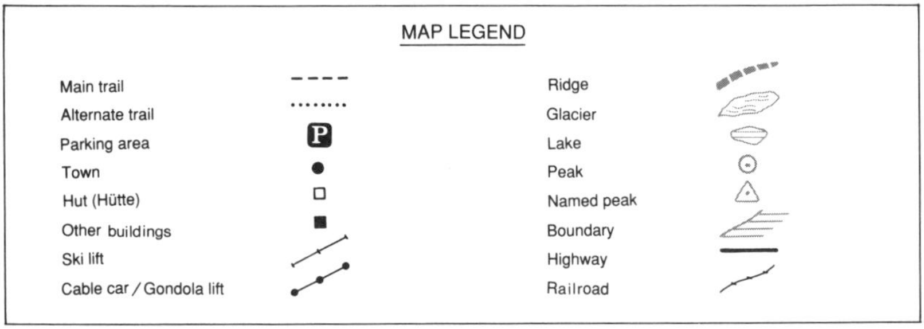

MAP LEGEND

Main trail	- - - -	Ridge	
Alternate trail	....	Glacier	
Parking area	**P**	Lake	
Town	●	Peak	⊙
Hut (Hütte)	□	Named peak	△
Other buildings	■	Boundary	
Ski lift		Highway	
Cable car / Gondola lift		Railroad	

INTRODUCTION

Nowhere in the world can so much varied hiking be found in such a concentrated area as in the European Alps. Hiking in France to the west and in Slovenia to the east are vastly different experiences, but only about 1000 km (620 miles) separate these two countries. Between them rise the Alps of Switzerland, Liechtenstein, Germany, Italy, and Austria—countries with their own customs, history, forms of government, architecture, and geographic and ethnic features. Just compare the vast differences between cities like Zürich and Grenoble, or Zermatt

Trail in the Brenta Dolomites (Hike No. 91)

and Kitzbühel; yet they are only a few hours apart. Proximity and variety are the words that best sum up hiking in the Alps.

When I first visited the Alps more than forty years ago, I had many questions that are as pertinent for today's hiker as they were to me then. Where are the mountain centers? How does one get to the villages, trailheads, passes, summits, lakes, and glaciers? What are the trails like? What dangers are there? Does one need a guide? How long will a hike take—a day, a week, a month? Are the hikes suitable for small children? Can one find camping sites in the valley and is camping permitted above the tree line? What are the huts like? Can one pick the flowers and drink the water? At that time, there were few guidebooks like this one which provided answers to such practical, essential questions.

This guidebook has two purposes: to provide basic information on what you will find while hiking in the Alps, and to encourage you to go out and find it. I hope that our photographs, descriptions, and maps will both tempt you to go there and help you clarify your attitude toward the mountains. Even after forty years of hiking, I'm still astonished by what I see, because there is no end to understanding and appreciating nature. For me, mountains offer not only the discovery of a very small part of some country or region, but the discovery of myself as well. Ira Spring, Pat, and their daughter, Vicky, who have been hiking and photographing all over the world for decades, share this approach. In our descriptions of trails—researched by all of us—we point out highlights, curiosities, and general landmarks; but we stop there. Do not expect minute descriptions of every twist and turn in the trail, the name of every mountain peak seen from the summits, or descriptions of all the wild flowers. These are things for you to discover for yourself by using this and other books and good maps, and through conversations with fellow hikers. We believe that our efforts will help you find the way on your own, and we think that only through discovery will you harvest the greatest amount of personal satisfaction.

There are literally thousands of hikes in the Alps; this book covers but 100. We go to main hiking centers, which have proved to be interesting, and we go to lesser-known areas as well. Once you have tried our hike, go to the tourist or guide's office and ask them where the other great hikes in the region are. You may find that the ones you discover are even better than ours. If so, write and tell us, and maybe we'll check them out for a future edition of this book.

With this book and the recommended contour maps, proper backpacking equipment, and common sense, you can explore the Alps from France to Slovenia on your own. Hiring a professional mountain guide is not necessary for any of these middle-mountain hikes. One other kind of independence deserves mention. We believe that getting *up* the mountain on your own provides a much richer experience than being whisked to the heights by aerial tram, a glacier-equipped plane, or even a helicopter. However, there *are* moments when even we recognize the advantages of mountain railroads, chairlifts, and even a bus or taxi to take you from one hike or village to another; and we indicate these throughout the book.

Transportation

The construction of major roads and automobile tunnels through the French, Italian, and Swiss Alps, and first-rate bus and train service, has made it possible to hike a trail in the French Alps one day and be on a trail in the Italian Dolomites the next. Travel by automobile is clearly the most convenient form of transportation in the Alps, particularly if you intend to stay in campgrounds. From there or from a hotel or a *pension*, you can drive to the trailheads easily and have a place to leave your extra gear. On the other hand, European car rentals, gasoline, and oil are expensive. Train and bus service (not to mention taxis), even to remote Alpine valleys, is wonderfully efficient and on time. Tourist offices, hotel or *pension* keepers, and people you meet can help you decipher the schedules. Public transportation may take longer to get to your next trailhead, but you won't have to worry about doing battle with the locals, who often practice for their next rally on the roads to St. Moritz or Cogne. So your choice of transportation is a question of your temperament, the amount of time at your disposal, convenience, and money.

While looking at this book, try to decide just what kind of traveling and hiking you want to do. Do you want to start off with a few day hikes to get into shape and acclimated, or do you want to set off on a several-day jaunt? Do you want to hike for a few days and then visit museums, castles, old villages, and cities? If day hikes are your choice, you are better off to center your activities around a major hiking center, and they are all over the Alps. If you want to do the GR 5 (Grande Randonnée, a 600-km traverse of the French Alps), then fly into Geneva, Switzerland, catch the lake boat to St. Gingolph, and you are at the trailhead (with jet lag) by noontime. Or you can fly into Munich, hike around the Bavarian Alps, catch a train to Innsbruck, hike in that area, and continue on to Slovenia and Italy—all by train and bus.

Camping out, particularly in the valleys, is more involved than staying in hotels, but considerably less expensive. The campground is often some distance from the railroad or bus station. And getting to a trailhead early the next morning may require a long walk or bus or taxi ride.

In Italy and Slovenia, major cities are often far from hiking areas. A bus will certainly take you up the valleys, but less regularly than in Austria, Germany, and Switzerland. Check schedules carefully. If you miss the bus you can hitchhike, take a taxi, walk—or go to the museums. In any event, don't let a missed bus keep you from hiking. Getting there is all part of the adventure.

Equipment

Boots are the backpacker's most important piece of equipment. In my opinion, most rock-climbing boots, with their stiff soles and all-leather uppers, are too heavy and hot for the well-groomed trails found in the Alps. Their main advantages are that they are close to being waterproof and provide excellent above-ankle support; but over long distances in summer, your feet tire and can swelter at altitudes of 2000 to 3000 meters. Recently, domestic and foreign manufacturers have addressed this

Hut keeper at Cabane de Valsorey (Hike No. 25)

problem and there are many lightweight, flexible, and comfortable models to choose from. Boots should cover your ankle bone and have a rubber lug sole. The best bet is to break in your boots before you set off on a long hike and complement them with a pair of lightweight sneakers for the end of the day when the return to camp, hotel, or *pension* may turn out to be a 2-mile macadam slog.

Two pairs of wool socks, an extra-large waterproof poncho that can double as a ground cloth or a drip roof for sitting under on rainy days, wool gloves and hat, a flannel shirt, a pair of shorts, a warm parka, a sweater, sunglasses, climbing pants of some kind (or knickers if you prefer), extra underwear, maps, a compass, a flashlight with extra batteries and bulb, a first aid kit, a knife, matches in a waterproof container, trail munchies, a paperback or two for the rainy days, a plastic water bottle—and your pack is pretty well filled. You may want to add a pair of binoculars, which will help you pick out the chamois, ibex, and marmots from far away. And some hikers take along extendable ski poles, which help to distribute body weight and can be useful walking downhill. My wife swears by them. If you are camping, take along a lightweight tent, a sleeping bag and pad, a set of pots, and a small stove. You can get good-quality white gasoline in Europe. In France it's called Essence C and is found in the *droguerie;* in Austria and Germany it's Rhein Benzin found in pharmacies. To carry it all, I prefer an exterior frame pack, although soft packs are still more popular among the Europeans.

Unless otherwise noted, none of the trails in this book crosses permanent snowfields or glaciers. By mid-July almost all middle-mountain trails are free of snow. However, snow patches may be encountered above 2500 meters in gullies on north-facing slopes. If you want to start hiking before mid-July, or if it has been a year with heavy snowfall, it is sensible to take along an ice axe and to know how to use it.

Camping, Huts, Hotels

One day you will be overcome by fatigue, the weather, boredom, or just the desire for creature comforts. A hotel is the answer. Small hotels can be found all over the Alps, with just bed and breakfast or with full "pension." Reservations are often necessary in high season. In some places rooms with breakfast can be found in private homes. Rates are considerably less than in the palatial hotels where Whymper and Mallory planned their adventures.

If you are going on day hikes, it is best to try to find a centrally located campground. These are readily available throughout the Alps. Many are open year-round, except in the remote valleys, which are often snowed in. Once you have exhausted the hikes accessible from the town or village you are in, move on to another region, country, or mountain range. Alpine campgrounds are well equipped with hot and cold running water (you may have to pay an extra half-franc in Switzerland for hot water), showers, sensible regulations—and lots of people during the summer months.

A great deal has been written about the European mountain hut system, and many other countries have imitated it. It is quite possible to travel from France to Slovenia and stay in huts all along the way. Most are constructed of wood, stone, and corrugated metal and are operated by mountaineering clubs; some are private. They are almost always strategically placed, at intervals of 4 to 6 hours' hiking time. During the summer months, they are looked after by a sunburned hutkeeper (or his wife) who is usually a short-order cook and an aspiring mountain guide. Many huts have solar panels for electricity, serve hot meals and snacks, and provide bunk-style lodging in dormitories. They are never cheap; if you are going to stay in more than two or three of them, it is worth joining an Alpine club and benefitting from the members' discount. The main offices of Alpine clubs are in major cities, the addresses of which are listed in the back of this book. However, in some popular hiking areas, there are branches of the clubs that have special membership provisions for foreigners, can give information about how to make reservations in the huts, and have a profusion of maps. Most Alpine clubs have reciprocal arrangements with American clubs, so take your membership card with you and you may not have to join a foreign club to obtain discounts. All in all, the huts provide shelter and fraternity; most important, they make it possible to travel long distances with a relatively light pack.

During my years in the Alps I've stayed in many of these huts. They are wonderful protection in a storm, but I've yet to catch up on all the nights' sleep I've lost. Someone is always talking, snoring, sneezing, singing, smoking, or getting up at 1:00 A.M. to start a climb. In season, the huts are overcrowded and barely tolerable. Still, a trip to the Alps isn't worth a schnitzel if you haven't tried at least one hut.

On some well-traveled trails the huts are so crowded that camping in certain designated areas is encouraged. I've come to prefer a tent, a bubbling stream around the rise, and a lookout toward the east. That way the sun hits you early and the ridges and peaks in front of you are backlit and a joy to wake up to. Once you get above the tree line, you can tent out almost anywhere in the Alps, except in some of the national parks. In these, no tents with poles are allowed, but you can bivouac within a certain minimum distance from the trail. There are of course other exceptions, and if you think you may be infringing on someone's rights, it's always a good idea to ask for permission to camp. If you can't speak the language, point to your tent, then see what happens. In any case, most of the time you will put up your tent in the afternoon, pull it down the next morning, and be on your way. You'll be alone with cows, sheep, goats, marmots, chamois, ibex, flies, mosquitoes, and the elements. Using a tent gives marvelous mobility. You can stop where and when you want; all that is required is a good, strong back. With a tent, many of our day hikes can easily be extended, and we indicate this in the descriptions.

Food, Water, Maps

One of the joys of hiking in the Alps is that you are never more than a day or so from a mountain village. Even traversing the French Alps or on the high route in Switzerland, finding food supplies only involves a hike down to a valley store, a nearby farm, or a mountain restaurant. There you can eat, for quality and quantity, such mountain specialties as *fondue au fromage, raclette, bauernschmaus, truite aux amandes, carbonara,* or *polenta;* drink the local wines; and go hiking if you are still able.

Since there are a lot of animals grazing in the mountains during the summer months, it's best to avoid drinking stream water. Wine, apple juice, bottled lemonade, soft drinks, beer, and mineral water are alternatives. If you must drink the water (and you certainly need it for cooking), fill your bottles from sure sources like the village fountain, a farm, a campground, or a source above a hut or refuge. If you must take water from a stream, you can boil it and hope for the best.

The hikes in this book are arranged from west to east and follow the crescent of the Alps. We start in southern France, proceed through northeastern Italy, Switzerland, Liechtenstein, southern Germany, western

Austria, northeastern Italy, and finish in western Slovenia. Each of our hike descriptions contains the name of the relevant map and its publisher. While it is a good idea to buy these maps ahead of time at a bookstore or at the office of an Alpine club in a large city, they can also be purchased in village kiosks or even at some local tourist offices. European Alpine contour maps are probably the best in the world. These are on a scale of 1:50,000, but some are 1:25,000, which means 1 centimeter on the map equals 250 meters on the ground. The spelling of all place names in this book is taken directly from the recommended map(s) for each hike. In hikes that take place near border areas, there may be variations in the spelling.

For more difficult or sustained hikes, trail information and weather reports can be obtained from local guides' bureaus and tourist offices. If you are up in the mountains and passing a hut, you can always ask the hut-keeper about weather reports, trail conditions, and how long it should take to get where you want to go. You can also ask farmers, shepherds, or other hikers and climbers for information. Europeans are proud of the fact that they can converse in several languages, even if not fluently, so you should have little trouble making yourself understood.

Pollution

Leave your camp cleaner than you found it. Carry out trash, tin cans, and garbage. As of this writing there are no emission devices on European cars, but Alpine clubs and nature organizations in the Alps have finally launched serious anti-pollution campaigns, particularly among hikers and tourists. As a result, within the past few years the high passes, favorite camping and picnic sites, and even the huts are cleaner and more agreeable. Being a guest in the Alps requires you to treat these unique surroundings with a lot of respect.

Distances

In the Alps, trail signs indicate estimated hiking times, never distances; so depending on which country you are in, a sign will say: "h2, m30," "std 2, min 30," or just "2.30"—meaning 2 hours 30 minutes is the estimated hiking time. Except in Italy, where maps are generally imprecise and out of date, these estimates are usually accurate and reflect the average hiker's time; but what is "average"? We have found that in some cases a hutkeeper or restaurant owner will underestimate hiking times in order to encourage hikers to climb to his place of business. Consequently, in this book we have used our own hiking times. But keep in mind that times will vary depending on your hiking speed, weather and trail conditions, and the number of persons hiking. To help hikers who are used to distances and to give some idea of the scope of the hikes, we have tried to measure trail distances on the various maps. This is difficult; the numerous switchbacks and steep ups and downs make these figures less than precise. Use them with caution.

Landmarks

In contrast to the rapid turnover in ownership of American hotels and restaurants, Alpine establishments are reliable landmarks—often the *only* reliable landmarks. A hotel, restaurant, or private hut may have been in the same location with the same name for 50 or 100 years. Nevertheless, the publishers of this book must point out that this is by no means a hotel or restaurant guide to the Alps, and mention of these places is not intended as an endorsement of one or another of them.

Restaurant at Schärten-alm (Hike No. 63)

The first edition of this book appeared more than ten years ago; many things have changed. Houses, aerial tramways, roads, even villages have been built. The mountains, with avalanches and erosion, and human incursions have also altered the scene. Consequently, to revise *100 Hikes* has required a thorough review of every hike that was in the first edition. With a few exceptions, Vicky Spring concentrated on Austria, Germany, eastern Italy, Liechtenstein, and Slovenia; I revised hikes in France, western Italy, and Switzerland. In this new edition we eliminated the five Pyrenees hikes that appeared in the first edition because those mountains, by any definition, are not a legitimate part of the Alps range; and we added several completely new hikes to take their place.

As I noted earlier, hiking in the Alps is marvelously varied and trailheads are readily accessible. Many of our descriptions point out the peculiarities of each country or region. But while differences are readily apparent, similarities are not quite so obvious. I'm referring to the people who live in the mountains. Although sometimes reticent, mountain folk, wherever they live, are almost always friendly. From June until October (the best hiking season), they are up in the *alpages* (mountain pastures), farming and grazing their sheep, cows, and goats. They send their milk down into the valleys or prepare cheese for the coming winter. Some tend hotels or huts or have turned their barns into rural hostels; they welcome backpackers with pleasure. They are living on their land in their country, and as foreigners we must respect these people and their customs. Even though you are just passing through, your contact with them can be a worthwhile experience. Your visit frequently offers them a pleasant respite from the hard physical work that never ends. Communication of basic needs and ideas is always possible. If you don't speak their language, bring into play your acting skills. The people may shake with laughter, but you will have communicated.

*The Mer de Glace and the Chamonix Needles from Lac Blanc Trail
(Hike No. 12)*

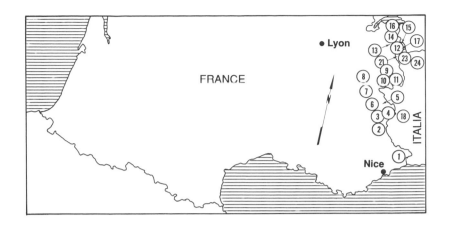

FRANCE

F ine hiking trails, well marked and maintained, lace all of France.
But the 10,000- to 15,000-foot-high summits, glaciers, and high
mountain passes are mostly found in the southeastern part of the country. Roughly, the French Alps stretch from Grenoble east to the Swiss
and Italian borders. The Vosges and the Jura mountains are the foothills
to the French Alps; while the Maritime Alps, which curve around like a
croissant, protect Mediterranean cities such as Cannes, Nice, Menton,
and others from the cold winds blowing off high northern summits and
down the long glacial valleys. The summits in the Maritimes are lower,
the trails are less frequented, and the terrain can be very dry, rugged,
and rocky.

There are marked cultural and social differences between the southern
and northern Alps of France. The language and way of life in the Maritime Alps has been influenced by its proximity to Italy. Compared to the
north, tourism there has developed much slower. As far back as the eigh-
teenth century, the northern Alps were developed as mountain-climbing,
hiking, and skiing centers. Influences came from Paris, Geneva, London,
and many other parts of the world. Despite that, French mountain
people, wherever they lived, have always been fiercely independent and
have resisted change.

South or north, for the past fifty years, as young people migrated to the
cities, many Alpine farms have been turned into sites for condominiums,
ski lifts, and hiking trails; and many village homes have become secondary residences for "foreigners." Nevertheless, to the delight of the hiker,
vestiges of French mountain life, sometimes meticulously restored, can
still be found.

1 THE PREHISTORIC PICTOGRAPHS OF MONT BEGO

Round trip to the pictographs	**Loop trip 26 km, 16 miles**
16 km, 10 miles	**Hiking time two days**
Hiking time 7 hours	**High point 2549 meters, 8363 feet**
High point 2300 meters, 7546 feet	**Elevation gain 1150 meters,**
Elevation gain 900 meters,	**3772 feet**
2952 feet	**Map: D&R Massif et Parc**
	National du Mercantour

The 2000-year-old trail around Mont Bégo in the Maritime Alps climbs up to the Vallée des Merveilles, which is in a national park. The complete tour, on the GR 52, can take several days; but a long day hike to the pictographs, located in a high desolate valley, is a rewarding experience.

The best estimates date the pictographs at between 2500 and 1500 B.C. It's not clear whether the people who made them were hunters, herders, or farmers; but the place has an eerie atmosphere about it. When we first visited this park fifteen years ago, you could examine the pictographs at will; but so much damage was done to them that the park authorities have created a "zone" that can only be visited with a park guide. However, thousands of carvings lie outside the zone, so we went on our own.

You can catch a bus from Nice to St. Dalmas de Tende, a fortified village worth visiting; and from there you can taxi or walk to the trailhead. If you are driving, head for St. Dalmas de Tende and from there pick up the route going into the Roya river valley, direction Casterine. Leave your car in one of the parking lots near the Lac des Mesches and from there walk back a few meters and climb a narrow, rough road. At marker 89 the trail branches steeply to the right, marked "PAR VALLON DE L'ENFER." A distant waterfall and stream can be seen and ½ hour later, at marker 90, the road trail is rejoined. The road continues to the Refuge

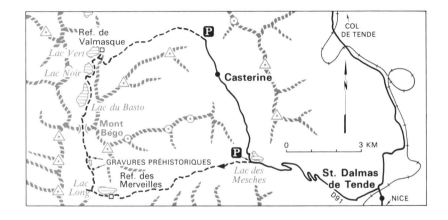

Pictographs in Vallée des Merveilles

des Merveilles on the side of Lac Long, elevation 2111 meters, 6 km from the parking area. From the refuge follow a well-worn but unsigned trail around the west side of the lake to the junction at the far end. Take the right-hand trail toward the rushing stream. It climbs up and down beside the torrent into the Vallée des Merveilles to a high point above a tiny lake, elevation 2300 meters. Here among the rocks and boulders you have to search for the pictographs. Most are small and faint, cut into the smooth sides of the reddish gray rock. Some are simple figures; others are more complicated designs of halberds and mysterious abstract lines. One can spend hours or even days studying this fascinating world.

The GR 52 trail, occasionally indicated by yellow paint slashes, drops down to lake level, follows the river upstream, and then with a series of switchbacks heads up over a 2549-meter col at 10 km. Then it switchbacks down to Lac du Basto, Lac Noir, and finally Lac Vert and the Refuge de Valmasque, elevation 2221 meters. If you don't stay overnight, it's a good haul from there back to the trailhead.

2   FOUILLOUZE
(Refuge de Chambeyron)

Round trip to the refuge 10 km,
  6 miles
Hiking time 4½ hours
High point 2835 meters, 9302 feet
Elevation gain 750 meters,
  2460 feet

Round trip to Tête de l'Homme
  10 km, 6 miles
Hiking time 4 hours
High point 2455 meters, 8055 feet
Elevation gain 580 meters,
  1902 feet
Map: D&R Massifs du Queyras et
  Haute Ubaye

You can easily spend three days around Fouillouze and never take the same trail twice. The area abounds in fascinating hiking. Stark rock spurs are set off by snow-covered peaks and passes. An interesting trail climbs to the Col du Vallone and the Tête de l'Homme; while a short leg of the GR 5 trail (Hike No. 16) climbs from the hamlet of Fouillouze to the Refuge de Chambeyron for a close-up view of the 11,119-foot-high Brec de Chambeyron.

Fouillouze is in the Ubaye region, northwest of the Maritime Alps. From Barcelonnette head north on route D 900 to the small village of St. Paul, about the last place to purchase groceries. From there, follow D 25 past Grand Serenne, and at 4 km turn right on a rough road marked "FOUILLOUZE, ELEVATION 1911 METERS." The hamlet has a friendly, well-equipped *gîte d'étape* (rural hostel) and two restaurants.

The high lakes trip (via the Refuge de Chambeyron) should not be attempted unless most of the snow has melted; other hikes in this area can be made in early summer, but they are most impressive in autumn when the larch forests have turned golden. All hikes start from Fouillouze.

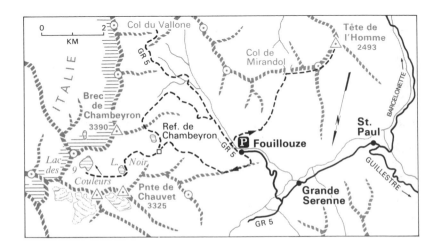

Walk through the village until you come to a church that has three bells mounted in its tower. Continue on for about 60 meters from the last house, where the trail leaves from the left. Follow it to the refuge, elevation 2650 meters, and stay overnight. The next day, hike over the schist and rubble rock past Lac Noir to the Lac des Neuf Couleurs, 3 km from the refuge, 100 vertical meters. It is claimed that at certain times of day nine colors can be distinguished in this 2813-meter-high lake beneath the Brec de Chambeyron. Return by the same route or, for variety, cross over the Pas de la Couleta to the valley.

A second hike follows the GR 5 trail on a narrow road by a primitive campground and then continues on a wide path to the Col du Vallone, which is very close to the Italian border. For the Tête de l'Homme hike, start out the same way but, a short distance from the campground, cross the stream. A few meters farther on, pick up a trail that rises steeply to the edge of the forest and an unmarked junction. Go right, following the trail through a larch forest to a high meadow and a superb view of the Pointe de Chauvet and the other Chambeyron spires. From the viewpoint, the trail becomes flat. First it contours around the hillside, then it climbs to the Col de Mirandol. Follow the ups and downs of the ridge to the summit, elevation 2455 meters, for a vertical gain of 580 meters. Return to Fouillouze by the same trail.

Pointe du Chauvet from trail to Tête de l'Homme

3   TETE DE GIRARDIN

Round trip 13 km, 8 miles
Hiking time 6 hours
High point 2870 meters, 9416 feet
Elevation gain 1120 meters,
    3674 feet

Loop trip 23 km, 14 miles
Hiking time two days
High point 2706 meters, 8878 feet
Elevation gain 2070 meters,
    6790 feet
Map: D&R Massifs du Queyras et
    Haute Ubaye

This hike to a tiny chapel on the 2870-meter summit of the Tête de Girardin yields superb views of the rugged spires of the Pic de la Font Sancte, the massive range of the Aiguille de Chambeyron, and endless mountains and valleys. A day hike or part of a two-day loop, there are three trailheads from which you can begin, and the trails all go to the same place.

Take highway N 94 south from Briançon, turn east to Guillestre, and then continue east following D 902, direction "COL D'IZOARD." At about 5½ km from Guillestre, turn right on road D 60 to the small resort village of Ceillac. From there, continue up the valley 3½ km to a group of farmhouses and the trailhead (with very limited parking), elevation 1750 meters.

The trail starts in forest as a wide wagon road, then crosses under ski lifts on groomed and graded ski runs. Magnificent peaks tower above the trail and at 2 km the trail joins the GR 5 and continues onto a 2400-meter-high viewpoint. A bit farther on is Lac Ste.-Anne, situated at 2409 meters in a bowl without an obvious outlet. From the lake, located 4 km from the trailhead, the route heads up and at 5½ km it reaches the 2706-meter-high Col Girardin. Climb the eastern slope of the Tête de Girardin to the chapel at 2870 meters, 6½ km from the road. When you get down to earth again you may want to wonder what it took to carry the materi-

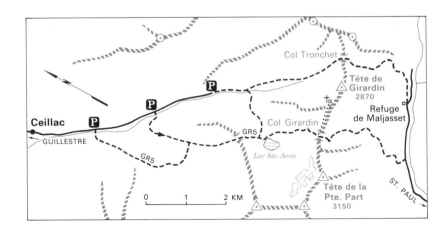

Brec de Chambeyron from Col Girardin

als up to this majestic summit to construct the chapel.

For backpackers who want to hike the two-day loop trail, drop down to the Col de Girardin and follow the GR 5 to the lovely stone Refuge de Maljasset at 1903 meters, a distance of approximately 5 km. You can get a hearty meal there and a bunk bed, or you can camp out in the rather primitive campground nearby. The next day, walk up the valley and through the village to the last house. To your left you will find stones marked with yellow paint slashes. Climb up this trail for a grueling 5 km over rubble rock to the Col Tronchet, 2661 meters. For us, and hopefully for you as well, the views make you forget the considerable effort involved in the climb. From this high pass you can see all the needles of the Chambeyron range and the entire left side of the Ubaye Valley, while to the northwest the peaks of the Parc des Ecrins are clearly visible.

Drop down from the col, pass a couple of lakes, and follow the trail along the river. At 1967 meters you run into a road that leads to Ceillac and the trailhead, 6½ km from the col and about 11 km from the Maljasset refuge.

4 ST.-VÉRAN
(Highest Village in the Alps)

Round trip 22 km, 13¾ miles
Hiking time 7 hours
High point 2882 meters, 9453 feet

Elevation gain 782 meters,
2565 feet
Map: D&R Massifs du Queyras et
Haute Ubaye

From Ceillac (see Hike No. 3) you can climb over the Col des Estronques, 2651 meters high, on the GR 58 all the way to St.-Véran, which will take the good part of a day; or you can drive around via Château Queyras. In any event, you will want to leave some time to visit St.-Véran, one of the most picturesque villages in France, which also claims to be the highest registered village in the Alps. The village, perched on the side of a hill, with pastures and mountains in the back and foreground, has been majestically restored. Chalets with extensive wooden balconies for drying grain recall the time when the land was extensively farmed. But the only revenue sources nowadays are cows, sheep, cheese making, and the tourist trade.

High above this already high village are two very accessible passes, the Col de Chamoussière and the Col de St.-Véran. During the summer months regular shuttle buses run up the road flanking the smooth pastures to the Chapel de Clousis, 2394 meters. Taking the bus will save about 2 hours' hiking time. But purists prefer the forest trail (GR 58) that leaves from the east end of town. Since we had a car and the shuttle

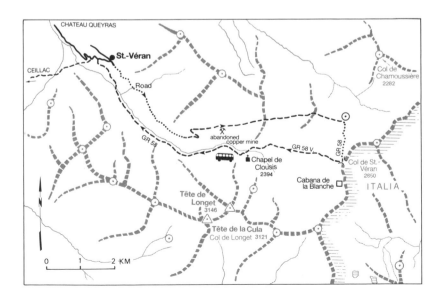

The village of St.-Véran (photo by Suzy Edwards)

buses weren't running in September, we chose to drive up the road for a mile or so and traverse as high as possible underneath the steep rock cliffs flanking the valley. We followed what turned out to be a sheep path over green rocks and slabs—the source for the abandoned copper mine below us. After about 1½ hours of side-hill walking we ran into the GR 58 trail rising from below. The GR 58 variant route took off to the right toward the Col de St.-Véran. We kept left, followed the yellow stripes, and were accompanied by the strident cries of marmots and jackdaws up the dips and doodles to the Col de Chamoussière, 2882 meters.

After admiring the views of Monte Viso (Hike No. 18), and the Italian valleys surrounding it, we traversed in a southerly direction on shale stone for about 30 minutes, keeping high, until we reached the Col de St.-Véran, where there were still more views—this time a close-up of the Tête Noire to our right, Monte Viso to the left, and the Italian city of Casteldelfino far off.

On the way down, we followed the yellow stripes of the GR 58 V., which joined up with the GR 58. In hot weather, you can head in the direction of the chapel, cross the bridge, and stay on the GR 58, which follows the river and skirts through the forest. If you are tired and the shuttle buses are still running, you can catch one at the chapel down to St.-Véran.

5   CHATEAU QUEYRAS

Round trip 14 km, 9 miles
Hiking time 6 hours
High point 2200 meters, 7216 feet

Elevation gain 1000 meters,
3280 feet
Map: D&R Massifs du Queyras et
Haute Ubaye

This one-day loop hike begins and ends at one of the most picturesque fortified cities in the French Alps. The hike can easily be extended to several days.

To reach the village of Château Queyras, follow the directions of Hike No. 3 (Tête de Girardin), passing Guillestre and then following route D 902 A to D 902. Park just before reaching the town, elevation 1350 meters. Walk back down the road several hundred meters, and near the sign indicating the village of Château Queyras you will find the GR 5-GR 58 trail marked "LAC DE ROUE." The trail climbs steadily up a steep forested hillside, with endless short switchbacks and occasional glimpses of the stone château below. At approximately 2 km, elevation 1800 meters, the steepness ends abruptly. Leave the main trail and follow the signs that point to the Belvédère, where there are two excellent viewpoints; from the first you look back at the château and from the second into a deep valley. Rejoin the main trail and climb to the 1839-meter-high Lac de Roue. Circle the lake until you reach a dirt road, where you leave both trails and begin to follow a road. There are fine views of the Côte Belle Crête des Oules punctuating the horizon. Proceed to the quaint village of Souliers at 4 km, elevation 1700 meters, where there is a *gîte d'étape* (hostel) where you can get a farm meal if you are hungry and a bunk bed if tired.

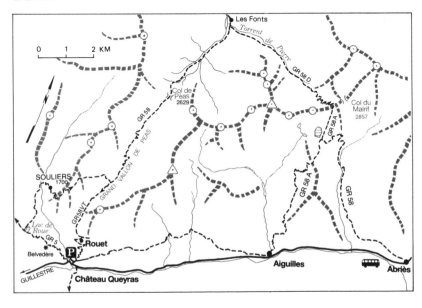

Château Queyras

At the edge of Souliers find the GR 58 trailhead marked "AIGUILLES." Follow this trail up a green shoulder of a ridge to 2200 meters, then contour around a steep hillside and descend into the Grand Vallon de Pèas to another road at 8 km, elevation 2078 meters. This is the dividing point between the short and long hikes. The short loop follows the road down the valley to Rouet at 12 km, and then by trail it descends to Château Queyras.

Although we have not hiked the longer loop, it appears to be a tour through delightfully green meadows. From the junction in the Grand Vallon de Pèas, cross the river and follow the GR 58 upstream, crossing the 2629-meter-high Col de Pèas. Drop down about 600 meters and spend the night at the hostel at Les Fonds, or put up your tent. The next day follow the trail (GR 58 D) beside the Torrent de Pierre for a 3- to 4-hour climb to the Col du Malrif. Just below the col, pick up the GR 58 A, which after about 1 km joins up with the GR 58. At this point you have to decide whether to head down to the village of Aiguilles on the "A" trail or take the longer GR 58 trail to Abriès. Whatever your choice, it is an easy walk or bus ride back to the big stone château. Incidentally, if the weather turns bad, there is a new geological museum at Château Queyras that is worth a visit.

6   LAC DE L'EYCHAUDA
(Ecrins National Park)

Round trip 8 km, 5 miles
Hiking time 2 hours up,
  1½ hours down
High point 2512 meters, 2526 feet

Elevation gain 770 meters,
  2526 feet
Map: D&R Massifs Ecrins Haut
  Dauphiné

The Lac de l'Eychauda is an excellent example of a lake carved out of a mountain by a glacier. The rocks by its sides are polished and scratched by the movement of ice. The water is silt-gray, but unlike most glacial lakes, this one has no visible outlet, despite all the water that flows into it from the Glacier de Seguret Foran, and snowmelt from the fields above.

Although the trail is in excellent condition, as are most of the popular routes in the French national parks, it is poorly marked. A good topographical map is necessary. It will help you locate villages, junctions, rivers, mountain valleys, and peaks, as well as the rather involved driving directions to the trailheads.

Go south on highway N 94 from Briançon, then pick up N 994 E at Argentière-la-Bessée toward Vallouise. Unless you want to do some shopping in the good cheese and sausage shops, or visit the ecological museum where you can obtain information about the Ecrins National Park, do not enter the village; keep to the right side of the river, direction Pelvoux. Continue on route 994 E approximately 1½ km from the village where you turn right onto route D 421 T marked "LES CHOULIERS-LAC DE L'EYCHAUDA." The paved route ends at 7 km at a *buvette* (bar) at an area called Les Chambran at 1719 meters. It is best to park there and continue by foot up the dirt road for about 1½ km. Then follow the steepening GR 54 trail up the valley. This main trail branches off to the right

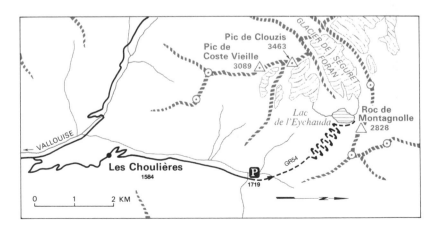

Lac de l'Eychauda

just after an area called Chalet de Riou. Keep left and after a final series of switchbacks at 4 km, elevation 2512 meters, the trail tops a rocky ridge. From there descend to the lake, which is only a few meters farther.

For a better view of the lake and the Glacier de Seguret Foran, go over the rocky knoll to the right and follow a well-defined trail another kilometer, switchbacking to the top of the craggy lake rim.

Trail to Refuge de la Pilatte

7 VENEON TORRENT
(Ecrins National Park)

Round trip 18 km, 11 miles
Hiking time 6½ hours
High point 2577 meters, 8553 feet

Elevation gain 864 meters,
 2834 feet
Map: D&R Massifs Ecrins Haut
 Dauphiné

Although this hike along a torrent to the Refuge de la Pilatte can be done in one day, if time permits you will be happy you extended it to two or,

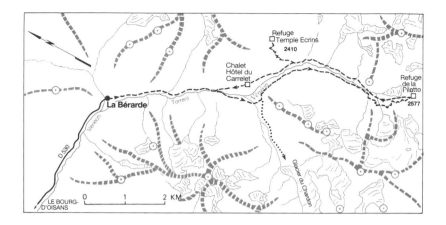

with glacier side trips, three days. There are about twelve glaciers in a relatively small area and the views of snouts, seracs, and crevasses are hard to beat. The trails are well maintained and the junction points marked. Keep in mind, though, that the side trips should not be attempted unless the snow has pretty much melted from the trails.

From Grenoble you can catch a bus to the hamlet of La Bérarde. It takes 3 hours and if you are made nervous by narrow, winding roads, this is not a trip for you. If traveling by auto, head for le Bourg-d'Oisans on highway N 91 for 5 km to Le Clapier. Then bear right (south) onto route D 530 and drive 26 tortuous km, on one of the most dangerous roads in the Alps, to the village of La Bérarde, the mountain-climbing capital of the Dauphiné region, elevation 1720 meters. Park in the lot below town.

Walk to the end of town and just after the Alpine Club hostel, pick up the trail that follows the Vénéon River. Many marmots live in this valley and you may luck out and see a herd of chamois as well. After about 40 minutes, cross a bridge to the west side of the river, and a little farther on cross a second bridge. To get to the Refuge de la Pilatte, 3 hours 30 minutes from La Bérarde, you must climb over a rock slide and several snow patches. The refuge, at 2577 meters, is perched on a knoll overlooking the Pilatte Glacier and a ring of craggy peaks. Because of the glacier and valley views, it is a sensational place to stay overnight; but be sure to get there early because this hut is a popular place, particularly with mountain and glacier climbers.

The following day, take the trail down the east side of the Vénéon Torrent. After about 1 hour you arrive at a junction with a trail, leaving to the right, which climbs to the Refuge Temple Ecrins, 2410 meters. The views from the refuge make the 1-hour climb up there well worth the additional 400 vertical meters. After lunch, in or near the refuge, return to La Bérarde (about 4 km) passing by the privately operated Chalet Hôtel du Carrelet.

8 COL DE LA PRA

Round trip 8 km, 5 miles
Hiking time 3 hours
High point 2257 meters, 7403 feet

Elevation gain 840 meters,
2755 feet
Map: D&R St.-Jean de Maurienne
No. 4

Lakes, snow-covered peaks, and soft forest trails gave us the excuse for setting off for two or three days of enjoyable hiking near Grenoble. In most years, the snow and ice disappear from the lakes by July.

The easiest way to reach this area is by taking a bus to the ski resort of Chamrousse, where the downhill events were held at the 1968 winter Olympic games. However, we wanted to avoid tourist areas; consequently we chose the trail that left from Frèydiere.

From Grenoble, travel by bus or car to the town of Domène. In the center of town next to the PTT (post office), turn uphill and take the Revel–Frèydiere road (D 11). After Revel, take D 280, and continue past several junctions another 12 km to Frèydiere, where you will find a restaurant. Climb straight ahead another 2½ km to the road's end at an area called La Pliou. Here at 1320 meters you will find a parking area and the trailhead.

The trail climbs steeply up a wooded ridge for 2 km and then contours for a while and leaves the timber to climb to Lac du Crozet, 4 km, elevation 1980 meters. It is a large lake with a small dam at one end. The trail circles the lake, climbs over the 2160-meter Col de la Pra, and continues a short distance to the Refuge de la Pra. Trail signs list the hiking time as 2½ hours; however, if you get there in 3 hours you are doing very well.

This comfortable refuge is an ideal base for walks to the cascade (waterfall) above the Chalet de l'Oursière near Chamrousse, to fine views from the Croix de Chamrousse at 2257 meters via the GR 549, and nearby lakes. For example, to the south are Lac Longet and tiny Lac

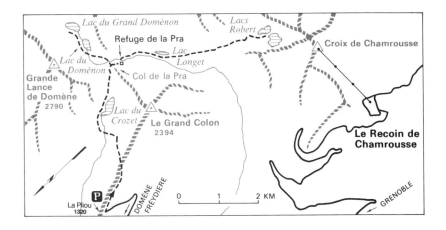

View from trail to Col de la Pra

Leama; and 4 km farther, toward Chamrousse, one finds Lacs Robert. To the northeast, within easy distance, is Lac du Doménon. We expected the lakes to be surrounded by luscious rock gardens, flowers, and green meadows, and indeed they must be during August; but when we were there one July, after an unusually severe winter, a three-meter carpet of snow covered everything.

9 TOUR OF THE VANOISE GLACIERS
(Day One)

Round trip 48 km, 31 miles
Hiking time 23 hours
High point 2916 meters, 9564 feet
Elevation gain 1765 meters,
    5789 feet
Map: D&R Massif et Parc
    National de la Vanoise, No. 11

Pralognan-la-Vanoise to Refuge
    du Fond d'Aussois
One way 12½ km, 7¾ miles
Hiking time 7½ hours
High point 2916 meters, 9564 feet
Elevation gain 1498 meters,
    4913 feet

This three-day tour of the Vanoise National Park glaciers is one of the
most cohesive and beautiful hikes in the Alps. Though days are on the
long side, you gain most of your altitude on day one; from then on you are
traversing, climbing, or descending slightly. This permits you to enjoy to
the maximum the views of peaks, valleys, and glaciers, which become
more and more spectacular with each hour. Because of the placement of
five major huts, you can travel with a light pack; and even if you decide
to bivouac (tents with poles are prohibited), you can still find shelter and
a warm meal in a refuge.

The tour starts just outside the borders of the national park. To get
there by car, take highway N 90 from Albertville (site of the 1992 winter
Olympic games), toward Moutiers. In the middle of town, pick up route D

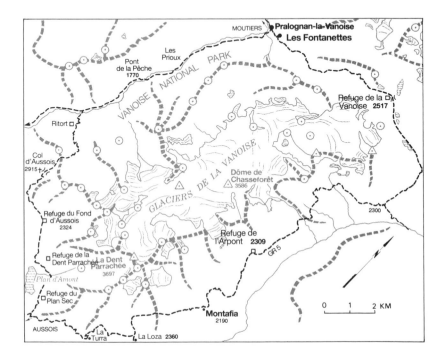

915, which leads to Pralognan-la-Vanoise. Or you can take a train or bus to Moutiers, from where there are four buses per day to Pralognan-la-Vanoise. A campground is located along the river and stores in town have everything you need for camping and hiking. You can get trail and weather reports from the tourist office.

If you walk on the road the 7 km from town to the trailhead, you must add 1½ hours and 350 meters of vertical climb to the first day. Otherwise, from town drive, hitch, or catch a taxi to the Pont de la Pêche, 1770 meters. Follow the GR 55, direction Col d'Aussois. The trail is large. You

Deer (diam) *grazing in a meadow*

Trail up to Col d'Aussois from Pont de la Pêche (photo by Suzy Edwards)

cross the river on a wooden bridge and begin a long traverse. About 1 hour farther on, the GR 55 heads to the right just before an area called Ritort. Keep left, direction Col d'Aussois, 3 hours. The trail leads to some old stone farm buildings surrounded by high weeds. Switchbacks rise to a buttress at 2160 meters—a fine place to picnic—where there are views of rock peaks, ridges, and faraway glaciers. The trail up to the col—the highest point of the tour—is over schist rock and marked by cairns. If the final pitch, which is steep, is snow-covered, be very careful.

At the col, there is a large white cross. Although you can see trails heading to the right, keep to the left of the cross and pick your way down over the boulders and numerous confusing paths. Once on the flat, the main trail is easy to find. It leads to the right and down to the small refuge, which is over the hill above an old lake bed at 2324 meters.

10 TOUR OF THE VANOISE GLACIERS
(Day Two)

Refuge du Fond d'Aussois to the
   Refuge de l'Arpont
One way 17¾ km, 12 miles
Hiking time 8½ hours,

High point 2461 meters, 8072 feet
Elevation gain 587 meters,
   1925 feet

Basically, this second day of the glacier tour consists of a long traverse between approximately 2100 and 2400 meters; but there is a lot of up and down and you may waste considerable time looking at villages in lovely valleys, hanging glaciers, high peaks, and waterfalls—nature in its most dynamic forms.

When you leave the Refuge du Fond d'Aussois, the only trail to take is down the valley. It crosses a stream, passing several stone farm buildings surrounded by cows and sheep. At 2208 meters you encounter a trail post. Keep to the left, direction Refuge de la Dent Parrachée. When the trail branches left, heading for the refuge, you continue straight ahead. Just above the head of the lake you pick up the GR 5 trail, which continues all the way back to Pralognan. Shortly after this trail junction, another trail branches off to the Refuge du Plan Sec. Stay on the GR 5. At the ski lift you keep left and go up the road marked Refuge de l'Arpont. You cross under some ski lifts, climb a short gorge, traverse high above the village of Aussois, and climb the switchbacks to La Turra, a fine plateau with wide-open views of the Meije and many hanging glaciers. It's time for lunch.

The pastures of La Loza at 2360 meters are reached by a series of zigzags, followed by a long traverse, a few ruined farm buildings, and views of La Dent Parrachée. You are still about 3 hours from the refuge, but from a scenery point of view the best is still to come. From Montafia, 2190 meters, you can see the city of Termignon down to the right. Fill up

Farmhouse near Refuge d'Arpont

Trail near Refuge d'Arpont (photo by Suzy Edwards)

your water bottle at the first occasion and fill up your senses with the views of two huge waterfalls and roaring streams that pour from the mountains on the way to the Refuge de l'Arpont. About 1 hour from the refuge you pass a small mountain farm on the right side of the trail. The farmer there has excellent Tomme de Savoie cheese and you may want to buy a small wheel. At the same time he may try to convince you that there is no more room in the refuge and you should stay the night in his bunkhouse. Ignore the pleas of this middle-mountain entrepreneur and push on, unless there have been large groups of hikers heading, like you, to the refuge.

11 TOUR OF THE VANOISE GLACIERS (Day Three)

Refuge de l'Arpont to Pralognan la-Vanoise
One way 17¾ km, 11 miles
Hiking time 7½ hours
High point 2538 meters, 8325 feet
Elevation gain 381 meters, 1250 feet

Edelweiss

This third and final day of the glacier tour encompasses just about all the variety to be found in the Parc de la Vanoise, or in the Alps for that matter. You walk close to glaciers, and there are chamois and marmots when you least expect them. There are glacier lakes and ponds, roaring

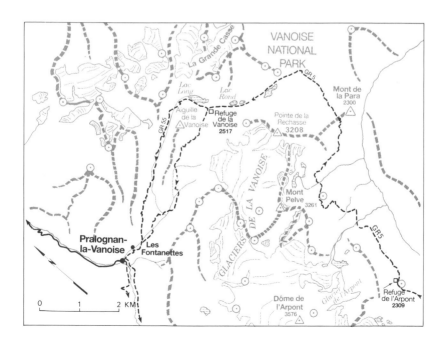

streams even at the end of summer, bubbling brooks, far-off 3600-meter-high peaks, lovely green meadows that in springtime are filled with flowers, and everywhere one looks there is evidence of glacial action that took place thousands of years ago, and continues today.

The GR 5 trail leaves from behind the Refuge de l'Arpont heading north. There is a signpost marked "REFUGE D'ENTRE-DEUX-EAUX, REFUGE FÉLIX FAURE" and the trail climbs to a low pass. The way is not too clear, but follow the occasional cairns. Shortly thereafter you arrive in a huge cirque. Centuries ago, this valley was covered by the Pelve Glacier. At the Mont de la Para, 2300 meters, take the direction Pralognan, 4 hours distant. You are standing high looking down onto several valleys and watersheds and a little farther on is an old blockhouse, a remnant from the Second World War. The trail heads to the left; Entre-deux-eaux is down below and you can see trails parting up and down the valleys. You continue across boulder-strewn slopes as you head for the col and the Refuge de la Vanoise, also known as the Refuge Félix Faure. Before and after the col there are several splendid lakes and swampy green meadows.

From the refuge, the easiest way down is on the GR 55 direction Fontanettes, which is just a short distance above Pralognan-la-Vanoise. But the most scenic route is to keep left at the refuge, direction west. Here the meadows, glaciers, and rich views tempt you even more now than they did when you started the tour three days earlier.

Butterfly on a thistle

Refuge Félix Faure

12   LAC BLANC

La Flégère mid-station to Lac Blanc–Col des Montets
One way 10 km, 6 miles
Hiking time 4½ hours
High point 2352 meters, 7715 feet

Elevation gain 535 meters, 1755 feet
Maps: IGN Chamonix, Massif du Mont Blanc, 1:25,000

An easy climb brings you to an alpine lake with a superb view of the Mont Blanc massif, the Chamonix Aiguilles (needles), and the Mer de Glace Glacier. From the lake you can also enjoy views of the Aiguille Verte and the Argentière Glacier and then, by hiking along the mountain flanks on the Grand Balcon Sud, you can rejoin the highway at the Col des Montets.

Chamonix can be reached by train from Paris (6½ hours), from Geneva, Switzerland, by bus and/or train (1½ to 3 hours), or from Milan, Italy, by bus via the Mont Blanc Tunnel (3½ hours).

From Chamonix at 1030 meters, pick up the trail to Lac Blanc next to the Le Brévent tram station, then hike in a northerly direction toward La Flégère. The trail soon joins Le Petit Balcon—the flanking trail that runs the entire length of the valley—but then branches off to the left, climbing steeply through forest until it bursts out at the tree line at La Flégère, elevation 1877 meters, in about 3 hours. You can avoid this climb by taking the *téléphérique* from Les Praz (up the valley from Chamonix) to the La Flégère mid-station, and/or continue by taking the gondola lift to Index. If you go only as far as La Flégère, you hike down in a northerly direction into a large bowl near the French mountain troop chalet, and then climb past the small La Flégère Lake. The trail becomes progressively steeper until it arrives at Lac Blanc, 2352 meters.

If you go up to Index on the gondola, the traverse across to Lac Blanc may be slippery and spotted with snow, except late in the summer. Fol-

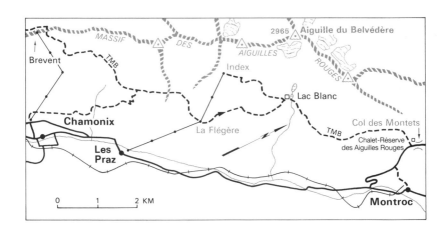

Lac Blanc and Mont Blanc massif

low the trail in a northeasterly direction into a large bowl called Combe des Aiguilles Crochues. From there, hike around a rock spire and make the long traverse that joins the trail coming up from La Flégère.

On sunny days, the Mont Blanc massif is reflected in the lake; at sunrise and sunset the views across the valley of the massif are extraordinary. Many people decide to stay overnight in the recently rebuilt hut, which is perched on the shore of the lake. To return to the valley, you can either retrace your steps to the tram station—an easy 1-hour walk—or continue farther along the flanks and enjoy mountain views from many different angles. The trail starts to the left of the hut and generally follows the landscape's contours; after passing several small lakes, the Grand Balcon Sud, as the trail is called, arrives at the steep switchbacks that lead down to the Col des Montets. You descend to a small regional park where there is a chalet with botanical exhibitions. Outside, along both sides of the road, are short trails along which the wild plants and flowers are identified.

13 LACS NOIRS AND CORNU

Round trip 9 km, 5½ miles
Hiking time 4½ hours
High point 2550 meters, 8364 feet

Elevation gain 600 meters,
1968 feet
Map: D&R Massif du Mont Blanc
et Beaufortain

Of the many hikes in and around Chamonix, there are at least two that one should not miss: Lac Blanc (Hike No. 12) and Lacs Noirs and Cornu. By traversing the Massif des Aiguilles Rouges all the way from the Col des Montets to Les Houches, you could combine both lake hikes in one day. But that is a long way and the only shelters along the way are at the Lac Blanc refuge-hotel and at Bellachat. So it is better to take your time and enjoy the sights. Both hikes are on safe, well-marked trails, the rugged glaciers and peaks across the valley are often reflected in these high mountain lakes (except after heavy-snow winters when the lakes may be covered with ice), and as you climb the views continually change.

The excellent jeep road from Chamonix to Plan Praz climbs 1000 meters and by foot takes about 3 hours. However, the Le Brévent *télécabine* (gondola lift) takes about 20 minutes, leaving you more time to explore and enjoy the lakes. Take your choice.

From the *télécabine* station at Plan Praz, elevation 2000 meters (restaurant with views), follow a graded ski trail to the left. In about 200 meters, after traversing under a ski lift, you arrive at a three-way trail junction. The left trail goes to the Col du Brévent, the right one to La Flégère. Take the middle trail marked "COL DU LAC CORNU." Although you will be interrupted by an occasional rock to scramble over as the trail climbs to the 2406-meter col, 3½ km from the gondola, the biggest hazard is not being able to concentrate on where you are going. The tremendous views of the Chamonix needles and Mont Blanc, Europe's highest peak, are very distracting.

Drop over the col about 150 meters to Lac Cornu, a rather large lake carved out of the hillsides by ancient glaciers. You are above the tree line

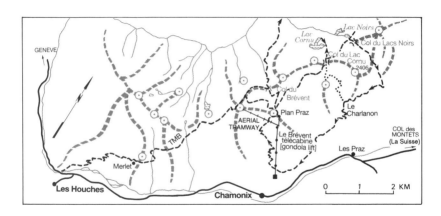

Mont Blanc from trail to Col du Lac Cornu

here, and the landscape is composed mostly of scrubby green bushes stashed between the rocks. The old rough trail between Lac Cornu and Lac Noirs no longer exists so, to reach the other lake, return to the col where the trail to Lacs Noirs is indicated. From the first to the second lake, via the col, you have to count a good hour. From Lacs Noirs you are about 4½ km from Plan Praz. To return via the tram station to Chamonix, climb to the Col des Lacs Noirs and back along the ridge to the Col du Lac Cornu, and then down to the cable car station. Or, if you want still more variety, you can go through the Col des Lacs Noirs and return to town on the trail marked "CHAMONIX PAR LE CHARLANON." You can do the same thing by backtracking through the Col du Lac Cornu. The Charlanon trail descends through the tall pines and as you descend it seems as if the valley is coming up to meet you.

14 THE CHAMONIX NEEDLES TRAVERSE

One way 21 km, 13 miles
Hiking time 9 hours
High point 2204 meters, 7229 feet

Elevation gain 1300 meters,
4264 feet
Map: Chamonix Massif du Mont
Blanc, 1:25,000

The Chamonix *aiguilles* (needles) are impressive from the valley floor and even more so from across the valley where the white glaciers help punctuate the spires. However, for a neck-stretching view and a good close-up impression of the granite rock—a favorite with mountain climbers—follow the trail that traverses directly under the needles. The deep gorge of the Mer de Glace (Sea of Ice) cuts the route in two, resulting in a lot of up-and-down hiking, so we felt justified in gaining our initial altitude by riding the Téléphérique des Grands Montets.

Take the bus or train to Argentière. It's a short walk from there to the tram. Ride it to the middle station (Lognan), elevation 1973 meters. From there drop down a short way to a good trail that contours around the hillside through a mixture of meadows and forest, heading south toward Chamonix. For about 3 km the trail descends and then reaches a junction. Take the left trail. It descends a steep gully to Le Chapeau Chalet—drinks, snacks, and head-on views of the needles and the Chamonix Valley all the way to Les Houches that will make you gape. On the way down, you'll soon find a network of trails. Be sure to take the trail marked "SENTIER FACILE" (easy trail). Find a trail marked "VILLAGE DES BOIS," which cuts off to the left and finally leads to a trail going south through the forest. Take that and eventually turn left and cross the Arveyron River on the bridge. Right after the bridge, turn right, following the stream for a few meters, and turn left a short distance to the dirt

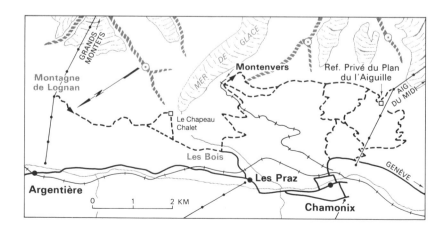

The Chamonix Needles

road. About 30 meters downhill on your left is a trail called the Chemin de la Filia, which goes up to the Fontaine de Caillet and Montenvers, elevation 1913 meters, about 11 km from Argentière.

At Montenvers, wade through the crowds of tourists and select the upper trail that climbs steeply over a 2204-meter ridge called "LE SIGNAL," with stunning views of the Mer de Glace Glacier as well as the Aiguille de Charmoz. You then contour around a steep hillside with a seemingly vertical view straight down the Chamonix Valley; then the trail joins the lower route coming up from Montenvers. From there, with more ups than downs, the trail traverses the Chamonix Valley and heads for the Plan de l'Aiguille. You can ride the Aiguille du Midi cable car down to Chamonix, or hike down on the Blaitière trail or one of the others that leave directly from the *téléphérique* station.

15   LE BUET

Round trip 12 km, 7½ miles
Hiking time 10½ hours
High point 3099 meters, 10,165 feet

Elevation gain 1769 meters,
  5802 feet
Map: Chamonix Massif du Mont
  Blanc No. 3630, 1:25,000

In the Chamonix Valley, the best views of Mont Blanc are from the summit of Le Buet, affectionately known as *Le Mont Blanc des Dames* (woman's Mont Blanc), the implication being that the "man's" Mont

Lone chamois along the trail

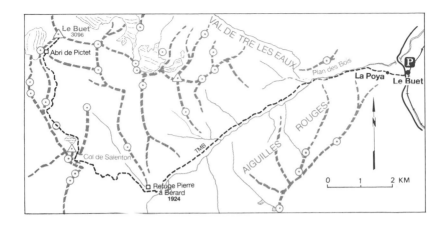

Blanc is the 4807-meter peak (highest in Europe) that rises majestically across the valley. Despite the description—a favorite among macho Chamonix guides—the climb up Le Buet and down in one day demands strong legs and good physical condition, whether you are male *or* female. After the climb to the summit, some backpackers prefer to spend the night at the privately run Pierre à Bérard refuge, 1924 meters.

Take the narrow-gauge train from Chamonix or Argentière toward Switzerland and get off at the station called Le Buet. Or you can drive up the valley through the Col des Montets to the hamlet of Le Buet and park at the station. Cross Highway 506, turn left, and pick up the trail after a few meters. Although it is rarely used as such, this trail is marked "TMB" (Tour du Mont Blanc), striped red and white. It starts out as an easy climb through the marshy hamlet of La Poya; it then follows the riverbed, bridges a waterfall, and near Plan des Bois crosses the stream. The climb up the river through the woods to the refuge is relatively easy. But it's a good idea to stop at this point and take some energy food, because you are going to need it. From the refuge to the summit the 3-km-long trail rises close to 1200 meters, so figure 3 to 4 hours. The steep trail leaves the refuge in a northeasterly direction, then heads almost due north and climbs over scree rock, schist, and through boulders left from old avalanches. You will know you are on the final summit ridge when the trail flattens out, like the dome of Mont Blanc across the way.

If the weather is good, you are going to want to remain on the summit for a good hour enjoying the 360-degree views of peaks, glaciers, and valleys in France, Italy, and Switzerland. No view from any of the tramways or any other summit in the valley is as majestic as this one that you have worked so hard to see. And the memory of this view will sustain you all the way down this rich, verdant valley that has been assiduously protected from any development.

16　GR 5 (Grande Randonnée 5)

One way 575 km, about 360 miles
Hiking time 1 to 2 months
High point 2801 meters, 9187 feet
Maps: IGN and D&R Chablais,
Faucigny et Genevois; Mont

Blanc et Beaufortain; Parc
National de la Vanoise; Ecrins
Haute Dauphiné; Queyras et
Haute Ubaye; Alpes de
Provence; Haut Pays Nicois

The dream of many backpackers is to traverse the French Alps—all the way from Lake Geneva (Lac Léman) to the Mediterranean Sea. It takes at least a month and since most people don't have that much vacation time, they hike a different section of the GR 5 each year.

In fact, diehard backpackers will tell you that the only way to do the "real" GR 5 is from Holland, where the trail begins; but we maintain that its most impressive section is in the French Alps. Starting from the lakeside village of St. Gingolph, the trail climbs rapidly into the mountains. It crosses high mountain saddles and pastures, small villages and ski areas like Sixt, Chamonix, Val d'Isère, Ceillac, and St.-Véran. It touches briefly the rail junction city of Modane and the walled medieval city of Briançon. After skirting the Mont Blanc massif, the GR 5 goes through the Beaufortin, a province famous for its mountain cheeses; the Vanoise National Park (Hike Nos. 9, 10, and 11), where animals, glaciers, and high peaks are breathtaking; and the lovely Queyras region, a mixture of calm valleys and rocky paths. Then the GR 5 crosses into the southern Alps, skirting the French–Italian border, and drops through the Mercantour region (Hike No. 1) where ancient tribes lived in stone caves thousands of years ago. On its way to the Mediterranean Sea, the GR 5 passes calm hilltop villages down to the hustle-bustle city of Nice.

The French section of the GR 5 is one of the longest and most varied hikes in the Alps and is certainly the best designed. In the past twenty-five years, its architects have worked to keep the trail away from big cities and up in the mountains as much as possible. The organizations that

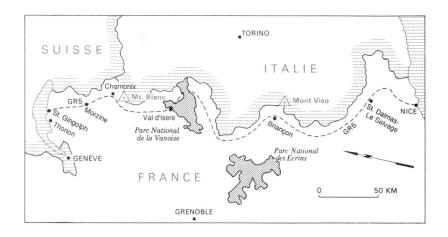

Point du Chauvet and chapel at Fouillouze

manage the trail have registered more than 100 rural hostels, called *gîtes d'étape;* in addition, there are private hotels and mountain refuges run by the French Alpine Club and the national park service, so there is always a clean place to stay and friendly local people who welcome you into their homes or hotels for a drink, food, and good cheer. However, you can camp out almost all the way from Lake Geneva to the Mediterranean, except in the national park section, where any tent with an armature is not allowed.

The idea behind it all was to encourage backpackers of all ages—French as well as foreigners—to frequent the French Alps, thus helping the depressed mountain economy. The organizers worked with local inhabitants, helping them repair facilities in their villages and financing an occasional *gîte d'étape.* Thus they made the GR 5 one of the most popular hiking trails in the Alps. Indeed, many of the trails described in the French section of this guidebook follow the GR 5.

17 LE TOUR DU MONT BLANC (TMB)

One way 160 km, about 100 miles
Hiking time six to ten days
High point 2537 meters, 8321 feet
Elevation gain 7117 meters,
  23,344 feet

Map: IGN Massifs du Mont Blanc
  3630 and 3531, 1:25,000 or D&R
  Massifs du Mont Blanc, 1:50,000

At 4807 meters, Mont Blanc is the highest mountain in the Alps. The Tour du Mont Blanc (shown on most maps abbreviated as TMB) completely encircles the majestic dome and its attendant peaks like the Aiguille du Midi, Les Grandes Jorasses, Mont Dolent, and others. Don't forget your passport because the trail skips in and out of France, Italy, and Switzerland, through six major valleys, over many moderately high alpine passes, through forests, and along rivers, roads, and trails. In good weather, the alpine scenery has few equals anywhere in the world; the huts, hotels, villages, and cities along the way make this six- to ten-day hike one of the most popular jaunts in Europe. Between June 15 and September 15, more than 10,000 people are on this trail: four-year-old children and seventy-five-year-old adults have hiked the trip with pleasure. Like any long loop hike, the TMB requires time and pace, planning, patience, and a good poncho.

But the tour is crowded. Groups from many countries reserve space in the refuges months in advance, and for this reason and for more peace and quiet we recommend that, if you are in reasonably good physical condition, you try the variant routes as much as possible. A guide describing these variants can be purchased in any good bookstore in the area. As for camping, you are permitted to bivouac pretty much anywhere between the hours of 6:00 P.M. and early morning; and because the refuges are crowded, many people camp near them, taking advantage of the shelter and hot meals they can provide in case of storms.

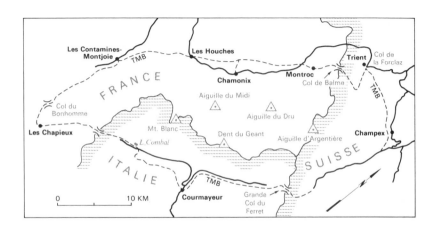

Les Grandes Jorasses from trail above Val Veni

You can start anywhere along the route. If the weather turns bad, you can wait it out in a cabin or stay in greater comfort in Chamonix, Courmayeur, or Champex hotels eating *truites aux amandes, fondue,* or *raclette.* Once the weather clears, off you go again. Whether staying in the refuges (be sure to make reservations in advance) or camping out, the company you keep will no doubt be international. The main stages of the route, with suggested overnight stops indicated by an asterisk, are:

1—Les Houches–Col de Voza–Les Contamines/Montjoie*
2—Les Contamines Montjoie–Nant Borrant–La Blame–Col du Bonhomme–Refuge de la Col du Bonhomme*
3—Refuge de la Col du Bonhomme–Les Chapieux–La Ville des Glaciers–Col de la Seigne (Italy, 2516 meters)–Refuge Elisabetta Soldini*
4—Refuge Elisabetta Soldini–Col Checrouit (Hike No. 23)–Courmayeur*
5—Courmayeur–Pré de la Saxe–Montagne de la Saxe–Lavachey* or Pré de Bar*
6—Pré de Bar–Grand Col du Ferret (Hike No. 24) (Switzerland, 2537 meters), Ferret–Praz de Fort or Champex*
7—Champex–La Forclaz–Col de Balme (France, 2191 meters)–Le Tour*
8—Le Tour–La Flégère–Plan Praz (Hike No. 13)–Le Brévent (2525 meters), Merlet (natural zoo)–Les Houches*

Aerial tramways, buses, and taxis can shorten or lengthen this famous trip. Be prepared for a few days of bad weather and plenty of views of high mountains and glaciers. For more details, study the recommended maps with care.

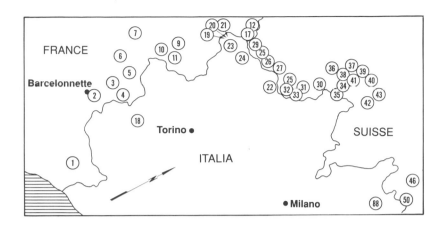

NORTHWESTERN ITALY

A little over a century ago, much of northwestern Italy belonged to the French dukes of Savoie. In the Aosta valley French *and* Italian are taught in the schools. In cities like Aosta, Torino, and Cuneo, and in villages like Courmayeur, Crissolo, and Saluzzo, French is still spoken, or spoken with a mixture of Italian almost incomprehensible to the outsider.

Despite occasional language problems, poorly marked trails, and maps that lack Swiss precision, hiking in this part of the Alps can be a very special and exhilarating experience. The valleys are less populated, the vast Gran Paradiso National Park (which borders the French Vanoise National Park) has many parts that can still be called wilderness, and tourism is not as invasive and consequently the wild animals are more numerous. But for me the real difference is not in the language or the land. It's the people one meets on the trails, in the huts, or in cafés. They seem to be more relaxed, laid back, and generous—friendly without being imposing. They take real pleasure in life itself, and that includes the mountains, food, and talk.

Unfortunately, the trails in this part of the Alps are not yet as well maintained and marked as in many other of the Alpine countries. The Alpine clubs, with very limited resources and many volunteers, do what they can; backpackers just have to use their heads, compasses, and altimeters a little more, and not be afraid to ask directions. The response will almost always be helpful—and you're almost sure to get a few laughs as well.

The Matterhorn and a flower field

18 THE TOUR AROUND MONTE VISO

Round trip approximately 30 km,
    about 19 miles
Hiking time two to three days
High point 2914 meters, 9558 feet

Elevation gain 2000 meters,
    6560 feet
Maps: North West Italy No. 428,
    Massifs du Queyras et Haute
    Ubaye

When you are in reasonably good shape and ready to tackle long distances, try this two to three days' delight around Monte Viso. Although this hike is mostly in Italy and its atmosphere is Italian, a corner of it sticks into France. Consequently, if you are already in the Queyras region you can join "the tour" by driving from Briançon to Abriès and from there southeast on D 947 to road's end and the Belvedère du Viso, 2133 meters. If in Italy, drive to Turin and then south to Crissolo via Savigliano and Saluzzo. Leave your car at the 2115-meter-high Plan del Ré hut.

The beauty of the tour lies in its scenic variety—rich valleys and forests, flowing streams and clear lakes, flowers in meadows and in high pastures, forest and rock trails, and several passes with views of Monte Viso, 3841 meters high, and hundreds of peaks in the Piedmont Alps and the national parks nearby. The five major huts along the way, although noisy with climbers and hikers, serve hot meals and provide bunk beds.

From the Plan del Ré, head south, cross the source of the Po River, and climb well-defined switchbacks about 2½ hours to the Refuge Sella (not to be confused with the refuge of the same name in the Grand Paradiso National Park). Unlike many Italian trails, this one is remarkably well maintained and marked with dashes of red-orange paint. After the refuge, near the Passo Gallarino, there are cairns to mark the way because, as is often the case, when the fog rises up from the Po Valley the trail is hard to find. Be sure to keep on the right fork at the pass. Shortly there-

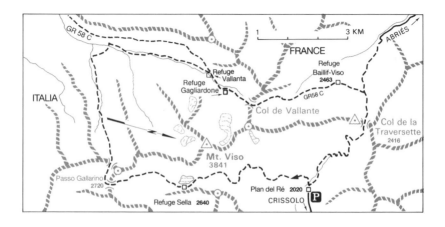

Farmhouse in Vallante Valley

after, cross the Passo S. Chiaffredo and then follow the stream over the rough rock trail into the valley. As you approach the forest there are some excellent sites for tenting.

The second day the vegetation and views change dramatically as you climb up the Vallante Valley, past shepherds' huts (*granges de souliers*), troops of cows and sheep, and the Refuge Gagliardone to the steep Col de Vallante. Many marmots have tunneled into the hills, and edelweiss, bluebells, myosotis, marguerites, and many other kinds of flowers can be observed. The steep trail passes to the left of the refuge and its lake and finally crosses into France at the Col de Vallante. Here you may find a lot of snow; you will want to exert extreme care on these patches, particularly if you reach them early in the morning when they may not yet have begun to thaw.

The hutkeeper at the French-owned Ballif-Viso refuge, at 2455 meters, serves hot meals from Easter to September 15, but it is a good idea to verify this before you arrive. We pitched our tent about 20 minutes from the refuge and, as the sun went down, we enjoyed French views of Monte Viso. The next day we climbed in 2½ hours back to Italy through the Col de la Traversette and down to Plan del Ré.

The trail to Col Entrelor (photo by Suzy Edwards)

19 THREE ITALIAN VALLEYS (Val di Rhêmes, Day One)

One way 35½ km, 22 miles
Hiking time three days
High point 3296 meters, 10,811 feet
Elevation gain 2914 meters,
   9558 feet
Elevation loss 2937 meters,
   9633 feet
Map: Parco Nazionale del Gran
   Paradiso, No. 3, 1:50,000

Val di Rhêmes
One way 14 km, 8¾ miles
Hiking time 8 to 9 hours
High point 3007 meters, 9863 feet
Elevation gain 1284 meters,
   4212 feet

Three major valleys flow into Italy's Gran Paradiso National Park: the Val di Rhêmes, the Val Savarenche, and the Vallon di Cogne. Dominated by the 4061-meter-high Gran Paradiso, the lower but impressive Grivola, and the ice-domed Ciaforon, hiking in the park is among the best in the Alps. The park is protected, animals are frequently seen, flowers in the forests and valleys are abundant, and you can pitch your tent down below or bivouac high above. The hand of man has barely touched these high valleys created by receding glaciers and erosion thousands of years ago; the feeling one gets is one of isolation and freedom. These four-star-quality hikes are for well-trained, experienced backpackers. Passes are higher and steeper than in most hikes described in this book, and they can be dangerous in bad weather. The most convenient access is from Aosta, which is about 35 miles south of Chamonix via the Mont Blanc Tunnel, and about the same distance from the Swiss city of Martigny. From Aosta there are early-morning and late-afternoon buses that will take you to Rhêmes Notre Dame, 1723 meters, where there is a small hotel-restaurant and campground. The trail begins in the square where the bus stops and heads through fields and up into the woods. In springtime, sumptuous rhododendron flowers light up the woods with red dabs, like a painter with a subtle brush. The trail is easy to follow with a gentle grade that bursts into an open meadow after about 2 hours, just above tree line at 2303 meters at the Alpages d'Entrelor. From there, indicated by use rather than by paint slashes or cairns, the trail rises to the steep 3007-meter-high Col d'Entrelor in about 2½ hours. The final pitch up to the pass is not only extremely steep but it is over loose rock. On the way we saw a herd of about thirty chamois and half a dozen marmots.

The view from the pass is spectacular. Many summits, lakes, and glacial tarns can be seen. Down the back side of the pass it is easier going. The loose rock slopes give way to green meadows and cow farms. At Orvieille, 2164 meters, a trail marker indicates a 1-hour walk down to Eaux Rousses; it took us longer because the red/white markings on the trail were erratic at best. That night we splurged and stayed at the new park-owned Hotel Paradiso and took immense pleasure in the hot showers, the wine, and the fresh pasta. There are more modest accommodations up the valley, but that would have meant another hour of walking.

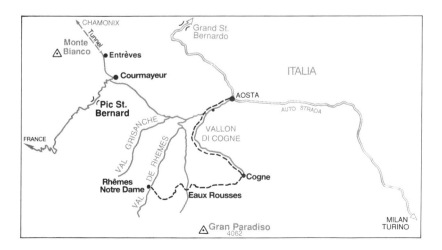

20 THREE ITALIAN VALLEYS (Val Saravenche, Day Two)

Val Savarenche
One way 14 km, 8¾ miles
Hiking time 9 to 10 hours
High point 3296 meters, 10,811 feet

Elevation gain 1630 meters, 5346 feet
Map: Parco Nazionale del Gran Paradiso, No. 3, 1:50,000

The trail begins on the other side of the road opposite the Hotel Paradiso. Once again, the rhododendron bushes and larch trees dominated the morning hours, and the rising forest trail was delightfully covered with soft pine needles. At 2303 meters you arrive at the first meadow, which stretches out from a ranger's hut. We were lucky. A group of boy and girl scouts from Rimini, who had been working on the trails, offered us fresh hot coffee; we reciprocated with squares of dark chocolate. After our brief picnic, we stayed high on the upper trail, which paralleled the long, green valley. Even though you cannot see the pass from there, the only way to go is upvalley. By the time we got to the fountain near the end of the valley, we were very thirsty. Take a good drink and be sure to fill your water bottles here because there is no more until far down the back side of Col Lauson.

At 2581 meters there is a trail post and a second trail goes to your right. Continue straight ahead. From there to the pass takes just over 2 hours and from there to the Rifugio Vittorio Sella another 1½ hours. But it is never easy going toward the end of the day when muscles are often tired. The trail is marked with prominent yellow slashes and an occasional yellow triangle with a number 2 in the center. That indicates that you are on a section of the middle-mountain Italian hiking trail that circumvents the Aosta region. Climbing this pass is not as difficult as the

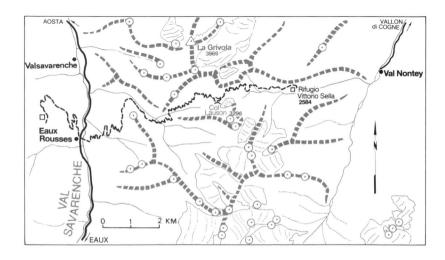

Pont Breuil

Col d'Entrelor, but it is higher by more than 275 vertical meters. On the way up we were pleasantly distracted by an edelweiss growing along the edge of the trail. True, they are a hearty species, but we were astonished that this flower had somehow survived the long, hot summer and the heavy foot traffic. At least we *thought* we were alone. We were sitting munching rat food and catching our breath just below the saddle of the Col Lauson when I happened to look up. Fifty feet above, looking down on us, was a chamois chewing his cud. And this was not the only animal we saw. On the way up and down, ibex and chamois were grazing all over the place, some not more than 20 feet from the trail itself. We had the feeling that we were intruding on their territory and should ask their permission to go by! Incidentally, the back side of the Col Lauson is steep and on a side hill. Under no circumstances should it be attempted in wet weather.

We weaved our way down to the Rifugio Sella, where we spent a comfortable, if noisy, evening.

21   THREE ITALIAN VALLEYS
(Val Nontey–Vallon di Cogne, Day Three)

Val Nontey–Vallon di Cogne	Elevation loss 884 meters,
One way 7½ km, 4¾ miles	2900 feet
Hiking time 4 hours	Map: Parco Nazionale del Gran
	Paradiso, No. 3, 1:50,000

At the Rifugio Sella, as in many huts in the Alps, everyone gets up early. Climbers are out by 4:00 A.M., and then backpackers and tourists are all trying to get into the restrooms at the same time in order to get outside before sunrise. At this particular hut there is a lot to see. At dawn, the ibex and chamois, practically tame, come close to the hut. They won't exactly eat out of your hand, but you can get within 10 feet of them, and that makes a great photo even for a "point and shoot" camera. But be-

Trail from Rifugio Sella to Cogne (photo by Suzy Edwards)

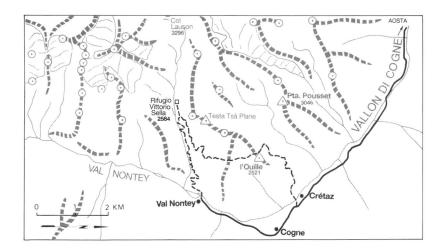

sides the animals, the sunrise seen from this hut is one of the best in the Alps. Faraway ridges become sharper and sharper, glaciers shed their grayness for fresh white, and the meadows light up like stained-glass windows. Behind you, the sun is racing down from the pass you descended the afternoon before, and finally you too are enshrouded in light and warmth at the very moment that the sun has cracked the ridge in front of you. An hour later, after capuccino and hardtack, pack riding comfortably, you are making your way carefully down the trail. By now the marmots are out of their burrows, eating and playing in the fields. The fear of man in this environment has disappeared, and what a wonderful feeling that is.

The trail down to Val Nontey, a small tourist village, is rocky but easy to follow. On weekends and holidays, the buses arrive from Italian cities and the tourists climb up the trail, most wearing low city shoes, with their children and picnic baskets on or in their arms, to "see the animals." Coming down from isolated valleys after two days into "civilization" to the souvenir shops, ice cream cones, post cards, and lines of parked buses is a shock. So much so that on this third day you might want to consider keeping left at the Rifugio Sella, flanking the Vallon di Cogne, passing below some 3000-meter peaks, and either cutting down through forest just below Cogne or continuing even farther to within a few miles of Aosta.

If you stay on the main trail, however, the walk from Val Nontey into Cogne, where you can get a bus to Aosta, takes about 1½ hours.

22   MONTE CERVINO

Round trip 12 km, 7½ miles
Hiking time 4 hours
High point 2516 meters, 8252 feet

Elevation gain 1500 meters,
4920 feet
Map: Kompaß Carta 87, Breuil
Cervinia-Zermatt

Late spring or early summer is the best time for this hike. The flowers
cover the meadows below the towering peak of Monte Cervino, the Italian name for the Matterhorn. The peak may be more dramatic from the
Swiss side, but in Italy it is still an imposing sight. It is surrounded by an
inspiring ring of glaciers, including those on the Dent d'Hérens to the
west and the long ice-covered ridge to the east punctuated by the
Theodul Pass. Since the Italian town of Cervinia is a major ski and summer resort, the cement condos, aerial tramways, restaurants, and other
commercial establishments may take you out of the hiking mood. But
pluck up your courage and try and see what has been left behind the cement facades.

Good bus service will take you to Breuil-Cervinia from Turin, Aosta,
and St. Vincent, where there is, by the way, a gambling casino, if that is
your bent. If you are driving, leave the Torino–Aosta *autostrada* at the
town of Châtillon and take the road to Cervinia, 2006 meters high. You
can park in the lot just after the tunnel or in the new lot next to the Plan
Maison–Plateau Rosa cable-car lift, which is near the trailhead.

From the church at the town square, go uphill about 100 meters and
switchback left, then right past the entrance to the cable-car station. At
this point there are two old trail signs that read "COLLE CIME BIANCHE"
and "PLAN MAISON-LAGO GOILLET." The latter is the trail you want, so
head left past the newly refurbished Petit Palais Hotel and follow a
rough service road that deteriorates with each meter of vertical gain. At
about 3 km, the "road" reaches some farm buildings situated on a green

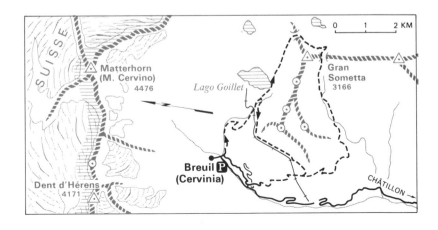

Ibex

knoll overlooking the town. In July, this knoll is covered with lovely wild flowers: anemones, violas, gentians, buttercups, and a few clumps of moss campion here and there.

Continue to follow the ruts of the abandoned road. Eventually, the trail crosses a narrow-gauge railroad that was probably used in the construction of the artificial lake. At about 5 km you reach Lago Goillet, the reservoir, elevation 2516 meters. Walk around the far end of the lake for the stunning view of Monte Cervino and the Grandes Murailles (great mountain walls), reflected in the water. From here you can make a short hike to the hill above, or take a tour around the lake beginning with the upper trail. If you do this, return to town by Barmaz, 2159 meters, and the Pista di Bob (bobsled track), and walk up the highway to the starting point; or you can descend in ½ hour on a newly made trail. And if you don't feel like walking at all, you can catch the *télécabine* back to civilization at Plan Maison. From the reservoir there is also a longer loop passing several small lakes, but in early summer the trails are often buried in snow.

23   MONTE BIANCO VIEW

One way 13 km, 8 miles   **Maps: Courmayeur 292; Massif du**
Hiking time 4½ hours   **Mont Blanc 2**
High point 2375 meters, 7790 feet

In some ways the Italian side of the Mont Blanc massif is even more dramatic than the French side. The Val Ferret and the Val Veni are far less developed. The glaciers and their moraines run alongside the roads that rise to more than 2000 meters, and the great peaks themselves seem steeper, darker, and more menacing than the Chamonix Aiguilles. There just aren't many buildings, which gives you an idea of the nature of the terrain.

This hike takes you along the side of a high ridge where you can absorb breathtaking views of the south face of Mont Blanc or, as the Italians call it, Monte Bianco. This exciting trail is part of Le Tour du Mont Blanc (Hike No. 17) but many people skip the additional climbing and take a bus directly to Courmayeur or they stop at Entrèves and continue by bus all the way up the Val Ferret to Arnuva. As we pointed out in our description of Le Tour du Mont Blanc, the variant routes are uncrowded and very enjoyable. It's true that you can have many of the same views by riding any of the cable cars that leave from the towns of Entrèves and Courmayeur, but the slow pace of traveling by foot above desolate Val Veni allows you to participate in the evolving views. Thanks to local bus service, you can make this a one-way hike from Val Veni to Courmayeur, or you can hike up a seldom-used trail to the top of Mont Fortin, 2758 meters high.

At Courmayeur take the Val Veni bus for 11 km to the end of the pavement. The trailhead is just across the stone bridge, elevation 1955 meters. Even from there the views are superb, and they get better. In 1 km the trail crosses a stream via a foot log; at 1½ km you reach an aban-

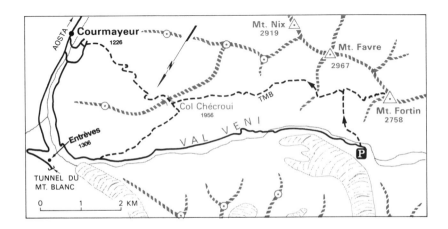

Bianco massif

doned farm and an unmarked junction. A look at the map is helpful at this point. One trail goes to Mont Fortin, a good alternate hike. The main trail continues up from the farmhouse to a 2375-meter-high shoulder of Mont Favre, about 2½ km from the trailhead. Little by little the mountain views unfold: the Mont Blanc de Courmayeur looms across the valley and so do at least five huge glaciers that spill off this massive cone. To the northeast, in the Val Ferret (see Hike No. 24), Les Grandes Jorasses dominates the scene. All along the route other views compete for your attention. At about 7½ km from the start, the trail drops down to the 1956-meter-high Col Chécrouit. Here there is a choice of two trails, each pleasant. The left one descends 3 km through woods to a bus stop on the Val Veni road; the right fork descends for 5½ km to Courmayeur itself.

Glacier de Pré de Bar

24 GRAND COL DU FERRET VIA THE VAL SAPIN

One way 21 km, 13 miles
Hiking time two days
High point 2554 meters, 8377 feet
Elevation gain 2066 meters,
  6776 feet

Maps: Courmayeur 292, D&R
  Massif du Mont Blanc et
  Beaufortain

Surrounded by some of the highest and most dramatic peaks in the Alps, this hike starts in a forest of larch trees, climbs over moraines and scree slopes, drops down into a glacial valley, and then rises to a high pass on the Italian–Swiss border. In season, the green meadows are speckled with wild flowers—yellow buttercups, rose-colored louseworts, tiny blue forget-me-nots, asters, and moss campion, to mention only a few of the many species.

    This one section of the week-long tour around Mont Blanc (Hike No.

17) can be done as a two-day excursion from Courmayeur. Hiking, via the magnificent Val Sapin, used to be a variant of the tour; but everyone agreed that the former variant should be the main itinerary, certainly a far more interesting route than walking the almost flat road from La Palud. There is, of course, a lot more climbing involved and an overnight stop at Lavachey is required, but it is well worth it.

The Val Sapin is rich in forests, water, and magnificent views. To get there, walk out of Courmayeur in an easterly direction on a short trail that runs into a secondary road. Follow the road to Plan Gorret, about 1400 meters, where you pick up the forest trail toward the Col Sapin, 2436 meters. A second pass, the Pas Entre Deux Sauts, is another 88 vertical meters above, and from there to the valley it is all downhill. Shortly after the pass make a hard left turn, direction Alpe sup. di Malatra. At Malatra itself, 2056 meters, keep to the left side of the stream and follow the signs down to Lavachey. The partly forested and flowered meadows of the valley floor are overshadowed by one of the longest, highest walls in Europe—the southern flanks of the Mont Blanc massif, punctuated by the needles of rock rising above the Glacier de la Brenva.

If you want to make this a one-day event, you can catch the town bus from Courmayeur that runs up the Val Ferret as far as Lavachey; but if you have a car you can drive still farther up the road to Arnuva and the parking lot, elevation 1770 meters. From Arnuva the trail, marked here and there with the red and white paint stripes that signal Le Tour du Mont Blanc, switchbacks up into steep meadows. The views of glaciers and peaks—Les Grandes Jorasses, the Dent du Géant, and the Peuterey Ridge—continually change with the gain in altitude. The hiker reaches the cairn marking the Italian–Swiss border at the Grand Col du Ferret, 2537 meters, 4½ km from the parking area. The trail continuing Le Tour du Mont Blanc winds down into the Swiss Val Ferret, but if you are not doing the tour, it is very time-consuming to return to Courmayeur via bus or train from Switzerland.

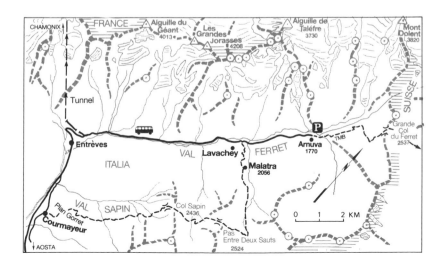

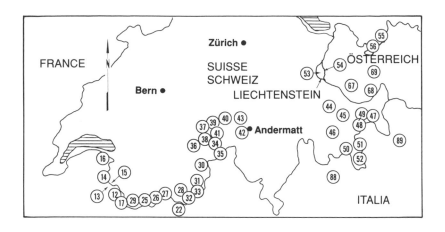

SWITZERLAND AND LIECHTENSTEIN

I t's probably true that any one-day hike in the Swiss Alps can be extended up to at least a week. Much of Switzerland is Alps, and high peaks at that. There is probably no other country where the trails are so well taken care of, the maps so precise, the huts so strategically placed and maintained, and the access by car, train, or bus so good. The tourist in Switzerland is well taken care of. Swiss tourism, with its long tradition, has become the "industry standard" by which other countries measure their amenities.

Besides many old and new ski, walking, and hiking areas, fine hotels, and luxurious spas, in the past 100 years there have been tremendous water/electricity developments in the mountains. Water taps are all over the place, even in the remotest valleys. In one case, water was tapped from French glaciers, transported underground to Switzerland, and the electricity produced sold back to France. It is claimed that it is possible to walk much of the high route (Hike No. 29) from France all the way to Zermatt, *through Swiss tunnels!* The Swiss have gone to some pains to try to keep these developments discreet and "natural"; but in some cases valleys have been irreparably damaged, whole ecosystems have been changed, and villages have been destroyed.

Despite the presence of "the hand of man" it is still a joy to hike in Switzerland. There are walking trails, hiking trails, and mountains to climb winter or summer. And it is still possible to find towns and villages where, outwardly at least, life is as it was 150 years ago. In some, there

Sheep grazing near Boval hut (Hike No. 52)

are no automobiles, and all over you can be sure that the trails will be perfectly marked, mapped, and maintained.

Liechtenstein is a small country located on the edge of the Rhine River between Switzerland and Austria. This 62-square-mile country has a constitutional monarchy government to run its internal affairs and allows the Swiss government to represent its interests for diplomatic and trade relations. The money used in Liechtenstein is the Swiss franc and the language is a German dialect.

Like Switzerland, Liechtenstein is an exceptionally clean and well-organized country. Trails are well maintained and carefully signed. Huts are well organized. If you have any questions about trails or bus service, or wish to make hut reservations, the tourist information offices are very helpful.

25   CABANES DE VELAN AND VALSOREY

Round trip to Cabane de Vélan
  14 km, 9 miles
Hiking time 7 hours
High point 2569 meters, 8426 feet

Elevation gain 937 meters,
  3073 feet
Maps: Martigny 282, Col du Gd. St.
  Bernard 5003, Courmayeur 292

The Cabane de Vélan, just underneath Mont Vélan, with its great view of the 4314-meter-high Grand Combin—a glacier-shrouded mountain—is one of the most popular hikes in Switzerland. The Cabane de Valsorey, underneath the Grand Combin itself, has a good view of Mont Vélan; but reaching the hut, which is more than 3000 meters high, is harder than getting up to the Vélan. One section of the trail is so difficult that we recommend it for experienced hikers only. For those capable of visiting both huts, at least one overnight stay is mandatory.

The trail starts in the village of Bourg St. Pierre just off the Grand St. Bernard Pass highway, leaving either from the bus stop in the village or a parking area where the trail crosses the highway, elevation 1632 meters. The trail follows the left side of Valsorey stream and crosses a farm

Mont Velan and Cabane de Vélan

road at several points. The road, occasionally open to public travel, is very narrow. At 2 km you pass a farmhouse and the road ends. At 4 km, boulder-hop a glacial stream, which can be difficult after late afternoon thunderstorms when it becomes a raging torrent. At 4½ km you reach a crucial intersection: the left fork climbs to the Cabane de Valsorey; the right fork goes to the Cabane de Vélan, the roof of which can be seen silhouetted on a high ridge with Mont Vélan behind it.

The Cabane de Vélan trail crosses Valsorey stream on a rather rickety bridge, and then after 7 km of seemingly interminable switchbacks up a green slope we reached the hut, elevation 2569 meters. We envied a party of Swiss hikers and climbers who were seated in the sunshine feasting on *raclette,* boiled potatoes, and white wine; we settled for some dry bread, cheese, raisins, and nuts, and enjoyed the views.

If you choose to go up to the Cabane de Valsorey, you must bear to the right on the way down from Vélan and climb past a group of abandoned farm buildings toward a tiny cleft in a fortresslike cliff that blocks all access to the upper valley. Below the cleft, the trail steepens and finally becomes a scramble, ending in a short overhang. A steel chain, firmly anchored in rock, hangs down the trail. By using the chain and natural footholds, you can scramble over the overhang with relative ease, but remember that descending is no picnic. Above the cliff, the trail is easier. It climbs across rocky meadows that turn into scree, then steepens until it reaches the hut at 9 km and 5½ hours' hiking time from the village of Bourg St. Pierre.

In winter, these strategically situated huts are section stops on the high ski traverse from Chamonix, France, to Zermatt, Switzerland (Hike No. 29). But in any season of the year, the views of high peaks and vertical walls from these two huts, and their solitude and relative comfort, make an overnight stay a very enjoyable occasion.

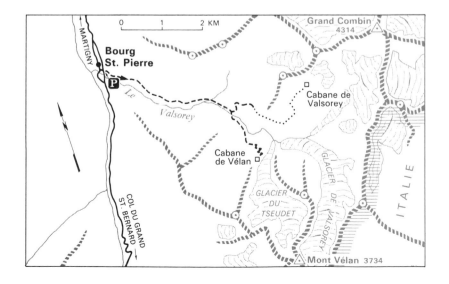

Tunnel under a waterfall on Lacs de Tsofèray Trail

26 LACS DE TSOFERAY

Round trip 20 km, 12½ miles
Hiking time 7 hours
High point 2573 meters, 8439 feet

Elevation gain 673 meters,
2207 feet
Map: Arolla 283

This is not a hike for the intrepid backpacker. You descend into the dim bowels of a 500-meter-long dam, climb up ladders to reach nature, traverse tunnels with huge quantities of water roaring overhead, descend ladders onto a catwalk, and finish the day with 7 km on a road—probably the most boring walk in the Alps. Much of what one sees at first is the result of man attempting to control nature, and as is usually the case it's a strange mixture of fabulous engineering feats contrasting with natural beauty.

From Martigny, catch the post bus or drive up the Grand St. Bernard Pass highway to Sembrancher. From there you go about 25 km up the Val de Bagnes toward Mauvoisin, 1900 meters. Four km from the dam, which has created the huge Lac de Mauvoisin, is Bonatchiesse, where there is a small store-café and a comfortable campground near the river.

The trail was routed through the dam itself! At 7:00 A.M., barely awake, with the sun coming up on distant peaks, you'll find it is no picnic to climb down ladders into concrete depths and then walk 500 meters through a tunnel, only to climb up again just to get to a trail; but the mountains beckon. On the other side of the dam, at 2 km, the road switchbacks up a green hillside, climbing 500 meters; at 3½ km it ends at a water diversion project. In good weather, there is no problem finding the way; but this would be a tricky place to be in foggy weather or on a stormy day, particularly since there is a stream crossing a little farther on that can be dangerous on a very hot day when the snow and glaciers are melting.

The trail climbs an easy grade. The lake is down below. You slowly leave the engineering feats behind and emerge more and more into lush nature. At 8 km, elevation 2573 meters, you reach the three shallow Tsofèray tarns surrounded by green meadows and speckled with lovely white pompon flowers that sway poetically in the soft breeze. From each lake there are different views of the majestic Grand Combin, across the valley. And if you climb the green hill to the east overlooking the largest lake, there is a view of the 5-km-long Breney Glacier.

We continued on the trail through a cleft in the rocks (take care on the back side of the pass as the passage is steep and over scree stone) down to the Cabane de Chanrion, 2 km distant, elevation 2460 meters. You return to Mauvoisin on a trail and service road below the cabane. This brings you around to the west side of the reservoir, making a loop trip of about 20 km.

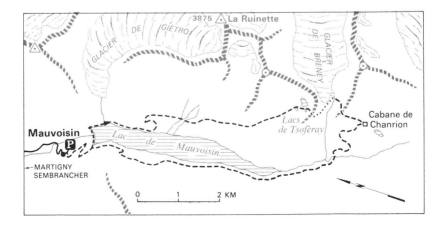

27 AROLLA—THE LADDER TRAIL

Round trip 10 km, 6 miles
Hiking time 3 hours
High point 2928 meters, 9604 feet

Elevation gain in 1000 meters,
  3280 feet; out 155 meters,
  508 feet
Map: Arolla 283

If you look out the left side of the post bus or your car window on the ride from Sion up the Val d'Hérens by the upper village road, you will notice tall spires of earth and rock, each with a large stone on top. Sometimes called a "hat shop," these sandstone spires were formed through centuries of erosion. The crowning stone protects them from deteriorating completely.

This is just one of the curiosities of Arolla, 2000 meters. The next is the pass, high above the village, to which you climb. This pass, called the Pas de Chèvres, is connected to the Cheilon Glacier by a series of vertical metal ladders. Climbing down or up these contraptions with a heavy pack, and in winter and springtime with skis as well, demands a cool head, steady nerves, and warm gloves.

Find the trailhead at the Kurhaus Hotel, which is above town. At first the way up is fairly steep, but it is marked with yellow slashes outlined in black. You won't get lost if you bear in mind that you must head uphill in a westerly direction. Once out of the forest of lovely arolla pine, the trail levels out somewhat as it parallels the Tsidjiore Nouve Glacier. You climb up by some ski lifts and at 3½ km the trail enters a small basin. Ahead of you is the Pas de Chèvres, elevation 2855 meters. The views are magnificent. To the south is Mont Colon, higher up are the rugged eastern peaks, and on a clear day you can see the tip of the Matterhorn. At this altitude the rungs of the ladders can be very cold, so put on your leather gloves and step carefully. If you want to avoid this passage, you can continue from below the pass to your right up to the Col de Reidmat-

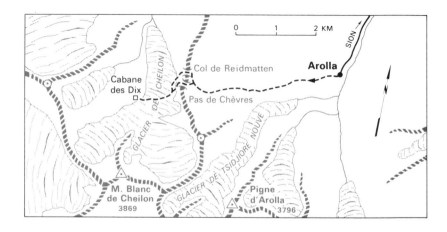

Ladder on Pas de Chevres Trail

ten (with the possibility of finding edelweiss on the way) and then down onto the glacier.

From the bottom of the ladder, follow the faint path marked by painted stripes on rock outcroppings to the edge of the Glacier de Cheilon, elevation 2700 meters. At this point the glacier is fairly flat, with virtually no crevasses. There may be some deep wells cut in the ice by meltwater; but unless the glacier is covered with snow, these wells can easily be seen and avoided. If the ice is snow-covered, stay on the well-used tracks.

Once across the glacier, climb to the Cabane des Dix, which is located on a knoll—a bit of civilization in a glacierscape, staring defiantly at the massive Mont Blanc de Cheilon. Spend the night there or retrace your steps to Arolla.

28   MEIDPAß

Round trip 14 km, 9 miles
Hiking time 6 to 7½ hours
High point 2790 meters, 9151 feet

Elevation gain 1135 meters,
3723 feet
Map: Montana 273

Sometimes it is a good idea to spend a leisurely day or two in the mountains just wandering around high plateaus and meadows, picnicking where one will and cooling one's feet in a clear lake. This hike lends itself to just that. From Sierre, which lies in the Rhone Valley between Sion and Brig, take the post bus or drive up the Val d'Anarivers to the village of St. Luc, 1653 meters. The valley road, cut into the cliffs and with many hairpin turns, is a marvel of Swiss engineering prowess; late in summer you can find wonderful fresh plums, tomatoes, and pears for sale at stands along the way.

There are two good routes up to the meadows, so you can go up one and come down the other. The first leaves from St. Luc itself. Walk the main street toward the church, but just before reaching it, turn left on a narrow road by a small park. Follow this road toward the bottom terminal of a T-bar lift. In a short distance, between two buildings find a wide path that climbs steeply. The trail passes a number of chalets, goes beneath the lift, crosses a road, and then enters a forest. There are numerous junctions, but once outside the village the trail is well marked with signs pointing to Meidpaß or its abbreviation, "MP." The trail climbs 300 meters and then follows a farm road contouring the mountainside. Near a farmhouse at approximately 3½ km the road intersects the trail; there are several directional signs here so there should be no problem finding the way.

The second itinerary begins up the road from St. Luc at the restaurant Le Prillet, 1690 meters. The most scenic route is alongside the waterfall, marked "CASCADE." From the restaurant take the trail to the right marked "CHALET BLANC," which you reach in about 1 hour. At the junc-

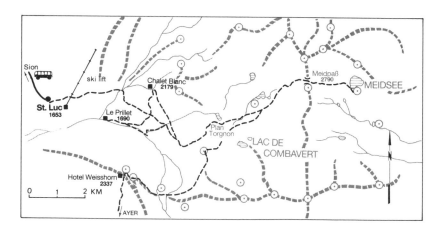

Lac de Combavert

tion, keep straight ahead and at the summit of the teleski keep right toward Meidpaß, 2790 meters. Since it will take between 4 and 5 hours to get up to the pass, you may well want to relax in the lovely pastures sprinkled with lakes and flowers that are so characteristic of this region.

Whether you take the route from the village or from Le Prillet, an overnight stay at the Hotel Weisshorn, which is located on a 2337-meter-high promontory with a commanding view of mountains and valleys, is a good option. The next day you can visit Lac de Combavert, climb up to Meidpaß (the dividing line between French- and German-speaking Switzerland), and even climb another 1½ km to the Meidsee, where there is a fine view of the Weisshorn. After all of that you can traverse across the easy hills down to the village of Ayer, from where you catch the post bus back to St. Luc.

29 LA HAUTE ROUTE

One way 180 km, about 110 miles
Hiking time ten to fourteen days
High point 3164 meters, 10,378 feet
Elevation gain (cumulative)
    10,640 meters, 34,899 feet

Maps: Massifs du Mont Blanc 1,
    Martigny 282, Arolla 283,
    Montana 273, Visp 274,
    Mishabel 284

The high traverse from Chamonix, France, to Zermatt, Switzerland, is a favorite trip of ski tourers in the winter and spring. There is also, however, a special summer high route for hikers, running through the Alps of these two countries. Some people claim that the summer high route—which crosses several passes higher than 2600 meters, takes one through fields of flowers, goes by old farms and lakes, and has splendid views—is at least as beautiful as the classic winter version. That's an open debate because the winter ski route, often over glaciers and through higher passes, provides some special thrills and even dangers that some mountaineers like to confront.

Some sections of the high route (or parts of them) are included in this book as day hikes; others go into new territory, some paralleling roads, train tracks, and cable cars. Many hikers do the entire 180 km on foot, while others take shortcuts, catching a train or cable car to eliminate less interesting road walks, or to gain altitude quickly. Whichever you choose, keep in mind that on a trip in the Alps that extends over several days, there is bound to be some bad weather—rain, wind, snow (even in the month of August)—and reliable equipment is essential.

You can start in France (Chamonix) or in Switzerland (Zermatt). The following itinerary lists the trip in classic day stages; but because of the route's proximity to towns, ski areas, and hotels, you can break up the voyage as you see fit.

1—Chamonix—Les Praz—Lac Blanc (Hike No. 12)—Col des Montets—Col

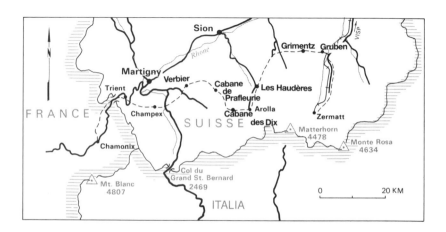

de Balme (Switzerland)–Trient, 26 km, 7 hours

2—Trient–Fenêtre d'Arpette, 2665 meters–Champex–Orsières–Verbier, partly by bus or taxi, 35 km, 6 to 15 hours (or 13 km by trail and 22 km by road)

3—Verbier–Col de Louvie, 2921 meters–Glacier Grand Desert–Col de Prafleurie–Cabane de Prafleurie, 19 km, 9 hours

4—Cabane de Prafleurie–Lac des Dix–Cabane des Dix, 9 km, 4 hours

5—Cabane des Dix–Pas de Chèvres (Hike No. 27)–Arolla–Les Haudères, 21 km, 9 hours

6—Les Haudères–Col de Torrent, 2918 meters–Lac de Moiry–Grimentz, 18½ km, 8 hours

7—Grimentz–Zinal (via taxi or post bus)–Col de Forclettaz, Gruben, 15 km, 7 hours

8—Gruben–Augstbordpass, 2894 meters–St. Niklaus–Täsch–Zermatt, 37 km, 7 to 16 hours (or 16 km by trail and 20 km by train)

Tsidjiore Nouve Glacier

30 KRINDELLÜCKE

Round trip 8 km, 5 miles
Hiking time 1½ hours up,
1 hour down
High point 2250 meters, 7380 feet

Elevation gain 470 meters,
1542 feet
Map: Jungfrau 264

The Lötschental Valley is one of Switzerland's most magnificent—a glacier-carved valley walled in by high ridges and peaks. On the south side are numerous hanging glaciers, on the north side are tantalizing glimpses of a large ice field, and at the head of the valley is Lang Glacier. The valley is so hemmed in that all the hiking trails are short. A trail from the road's end goes only 4 km to the snout of Lang Glacier; another

The Bietschorn

climbs 1000 meters to the Bietschorn Hütte; and several trails follow rushing tributary streams. The only trail of any length is Lötschentaler Höhenweg, a 10-km high traverse of the valley. But what the trails lack in length is made up for in scenery.

In the Rhone Valley, between the cities of Sion and Visp, take the road marked "GOPPENSTEIN," often indicated by a picture of an auto on a train. That's because at Goppenstein you can put your car on a train and 20 minutes later be in Kandersteg, where there is also good hiking (Hike No. 36). From Goppenstein, follow the road up the valley in an easterly direction to its end at Fafleralp, where you will find a huge parking lot, a kiosk, and the post bus stop, elevation 1780 meters. But before you get there you should stop in the town of Blatten, which is one of those Swiss villages that should be visited mainly because, with its restored wood chalets, the town represents what life was like many decades ago in an isolated Swiss valley. Fafleralp is a popular place and buses run there about every 40 minutes.

From the northwest corner of the lot, follow a concrete road that skirts beneath the hotel. Keep right at the fork and you end up at a small pond where trail markers are found. Take the trail to the right marked "KRINDELLÜCKE, 1¼ HOURS." The trail heads right, climbing through the woods in a series of long, easy switchbacks, which gradually get shorter and a bit steeper. At 4 km, elevation 2250 meters, you reach the crest of a prominent knoll where there is an array of avalanche control fences. The views are superb up and down the Lötschental Valley and across to the knifelike ridge of the Bietschorn. Even if you climb higher the views don't improve much, so you might just as well stay where you are and soak it all in.

To return to the parking lot, retrace your steps; but if you want to extend the day and the views in this relatively undeveloped valley, you can hike back to Goppenstein on the Lötschentaler Höhenweg in 6 hours 20 minutes.

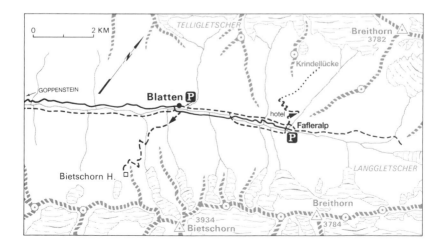

31 TÄSCH HÜTTE

Round trip 14 km, 9 miles
Hiking time 8 hours
High point 2708 meters, 8883 feet

Elevation gain 1260 meters,
4133 feet
Map: Mischabel 284

Variety is the best way to describe this hike to a typical Swiss mountain hut. Active farms, a quaint church, flower-covered meadows in springtime, large patches of edelweiss, stunning mountain views, and if you are lucky a herd of chamois—all can be found in this one hike that, probably more than any other, describes the Swiss mountain scene.

From the Rhone Valley city of Visp, catch the train or drive toward Zermatt past lush vineyards and orchards. Disembark at Täsch. Since automobile traffic is restricted in Zermatt, hundreds of cars and buses will be parked in the big lot. If you have a car, or can afford a taxi, you can save about 4 km and 2½ hours of forest hiking by driving up a narrow asphalt farm road to the church at Täsch Alps, and climbing to the hut from there.

However, since walking is both our aim and pleasure, for us this hike began at the train station, elevation 1438 meters. Go up the street, take the only right, and walk toward Zermatt for a short distance; then turn left onto a paved road, following the signs marked "TÄSCHALPS." This road takes you to a cluster of buildings at the edge of the valley floor. Find the trailhead between two old barns. The trail climbs steeply through the forest. Between the tall pine trees are views of the mountains and a distant glimpse of the north and east faces of the Matterhorn. The trail crosses the asphalt road several times before reaching Täschalpen, elevation 2203 meters, and its small church surrounded by pastureland. The year 1990, when we were there, was a dry one and it followed two relatively dry winters; so at Täschalpen the scenery was almost arid. But if the meadows were not particularly green, and the herds

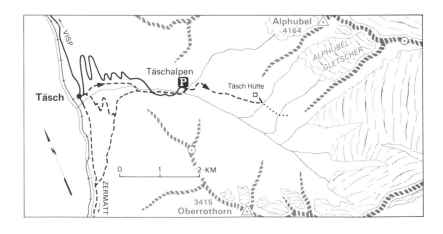

Täsch Hütte

of sheep a bit grubby, the distant views of the Rimfischhorn and other 4000-meter-high peaks were breathtaking.

Although the farm road continues up the valley, this is not the route to the Täsch hut. Instead, climb up a rough service road used by farm tractors that supply the hut. On the road, the Matterhorn has disappeared from view, but the Weisshorn and its many glaciers loom larger the higher you climb. After 3 steep km, you reach the 2708-meter-high Täsch Hütte, where there are approximately 40 bunks and hot food. The hut may well be crowded since it is the starting point for hikes to climbs to glaciers and high peaks east of Zermatt.

In early morning or late afternoon you may be able to see the herd of chamois that live near the hut. Wander around a bit and you may also find patches of edelweiss. Although this is a sturdy plant able to withstand almost any weather conditions, it, like most wild flowers in the Alps, is protected and must not be picked.

32 SCHÖNBIEL HÜTTE

Round trip 22 km, 14 miles
Hiking time 4 hours up, 3½ down
High point 2694 meters, 8836 feet
Elevation gain 1089 meters,
   3572 feet
Maps: Arolla 283, Mischabel 284

Old farm buildings in Hubel

In 1865 Edward Whymper was the first person to scale the Matterhorn. His ascension and the dramatic circumstances surrounding the climb did a great deal to make this peak the most famous in the Alps. That towering pinnacle dominates Zermatt and all the peaks in the area. The Matterhorn can be seen from many vantage points: from Zermatt itself, from Italian villages (where it is called Monte Cervino), or from faraway summits like the Pigne d'Arolla and Mont Blanc. One of the most delightful and lesser-known views, however, is on the trail on the way up to the Schönbiel Hütte via the tiny village of Zmutt, 3 km outside of Zermatt. The trail to the hut passes so close to the base of the Matterhorn that,

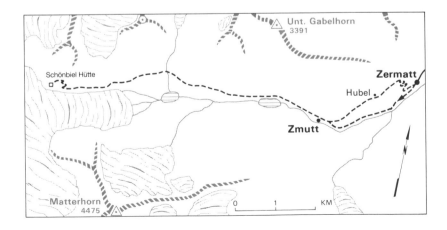

The Matterhorn viewed from trail to Schönbiel Hütte

like New York City skyscrapers, one can barely see the summit.

This hike can be a long day's outing or, better still, include an overnight stay at the hut. From Zermatt's railroad station, elevation 1605 meters, walk up the valley on the main street through town, staying on the right side of the river and to the right of the toll trail through the gorge. The trail climbs through fields and woods to a small cluster of weathered farm buildings grouped around a church. Continue up the valley, passing a small reservoir across from a complex of water conduits. With glimpses of the tortured Tiefmatten Glacier, the trail dips under a cliff, then up again onto a lateral moraine opposite the snout of the Z'mutt Glacier. Views expand dramatically, and one can discern the sharp ridges of the Dent d'Hérens, the Dent Blanche, and the towering Matterhorn rising up into the sky.

For about 4 km, the trail climbs gradually, passing under a glacier that literally hangs on the side of the Pte. de Zinal. Then the trail switchbacks up and reaches the Schönbiel Hütte at 2694 meters, 11 km from Zermatt. The hut is located on a knoll surrounded by glacier, with a superb panorama of mountains.

To vary the return trip, leave the main trail at Zmutt. Follow a trail to the left that climbs steeply at first and then traverses to Hubel, a photogenic cluster of farm buildings, before descending steeply to Zermatt.

33   GORNERGRAT

One way 12 km, 7½ miles   Elevation loss 1500 meters,
Hiking time 4 hours   4920 feet
High point 3090 meters, 10,135 feet   Map: Mischabel 284

Like all beautiful mountains, the Matterhorn and Monte Rosa can be
seen in many different ways from many angles: reflected in lakes, towering over an alpine village with green meadows and colorful flowers in the
foreground, or casting their shadows across high glaciers. This
Gornergrat day hike provides all of these viewpoints and more.
     You can get to the heights quickly by taking the expensive but amus-

The Matterhorn

ing cog railway from Zermatt to the Gornergrat, 3090 meters; or you can walk up *and* down. If you elect to do this you will be hiking about 24 km, with an elevation gain of close to 1500 meters. For some hikers, the cost of the cog railway may well prove prohibitive and they will elect to walk. By carefully choosing your way, it is possible to shorten the trip. For example, from the train station wander through the maze of narrow roads for 100 meters and work your way left, cross the river, and climb the steep hill at the far side. Once on the hill above town, the way is well signed. All you have to do is choose from the many trails: strong hikers to Rifelalp, the Gornergrat, and Stockhorn; others a shorter trip to Rifelalp with a loop return via Findeln.

Going up the cog railway is an extraordinary experience that should not be missed if at all possible. Sitting in the car clicking and clanking up the mountain, the foliage gradually changes, the snow comes closer, the seracs and crevasses on the glacier loom above and below. You enter a cold and eerie world that makes you want to see more and more. And you can! From the Gornergrat you can go even higher, swinging in a cable car over the snowfields and glaciers to the summit of the Stockhorn, where the views of the peaks are spectacular.

However, you may want to take the cable car back down to the Gornergrat, because hiking down from the Stockhorn can be tricky and, depending on conditions, may require mountaineering skills and equipment. The Gornergrat downhill trail starts on the Monte Rosa side of the railroad tracks. It descends steeply through arctic tundra-type vegetation, past a small tarn, and then past breathtaking views of the massive Gorner Glacier, which flows from Monte Rosa and the Breithorn. At the Rifelalp Hotel and restaurant, the trail divides. Take the first trail on the right, above the hotel, and begin the long traverse through weathered larch trees to another intersection. Here, follow the signs to Findeln. This requires a descent and then a climb back up to the village's cluster of traditional slate-roofed farmhouses and barns, interspersed with mountain cafés. From Findeln, it's an easy descent back to Zermatt. You will have spent a memorable day.

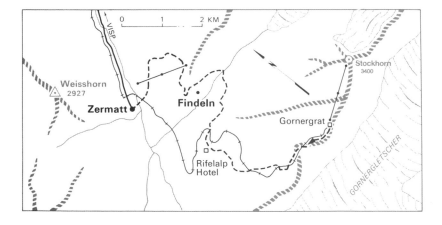

34   GROßER ALETSCH GLACIER

One way 14 km, 9 miles
Hiking time 4 hours
High point 2893 meters, 9489 feet
Elevation gain 200 meters, 656 feet

Elevation loss 1180 meters,
3870 feet
Map: Jungfrau 264

Sixteen miles long, the Aletsch is the longest glacier in the Alps. Chamois, lush mountain views, and the deep green meadows of the Bettmeralp can be seen between the three major cable cars and chairlifts that rise up from the Goms valley between Brig and the Grimselpass. Unfortunately, without going out on the glacier itself, there are no long trails, but the views are still there. With its many hotels and huts, this area is a good place to spend a night or two, watch sunrises and sunsets, and observe the animals. To do this, you can use uphill transportation to advantage: you gain altitude rapidly and exchange solitude for variety of the landscape and popularity of the area. In addition, lifts greatly facilitate loop trips which, for some hikers, might otherwise be too strenuous. Buy the more economical round-trip lift ticket.

From the Rhone Valley city of Brig, drive or take the train to Fiesch and catch the cable car to a 2893-meter shoulder of the Eggishorn. On a clear day, you can pick out the Matterhorn; but even more striking is that the lengthy Aletsch Glacier, which flows out of the Jungfrau, makes a wide turn below the Eggishorn from where the hike starts. Before leaving, be sure to ask if there is ice and snow on the trail. If there is, and you are not properly equipped, don't take a chance. Return on the cable car to the middle terminal.

From the upper terminal, follow the ridge a short distance to the north,

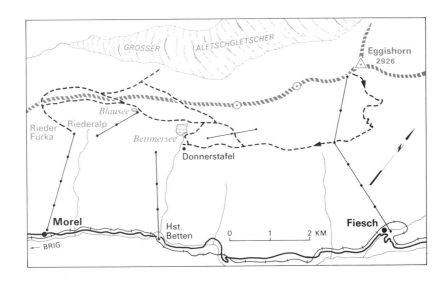

Großer Aletsch Glacier near Blausee

then take a steep trail, which switchbacks down a rocky hillside, until you reach a service road and hotel. The service road takes you west, back to the middle terminal of the cable car, for a hike of approximately 4 km. From there follow the ups and downs of the service road to the 1948-meter-high village of Donnerstafel at 8 km. Either go all the way to Donnerstafel and climb back up to the shallow lake of Bettmersee, or find a trail to the right crossing under a chairlift. Continue on to Blausee, a smaller lake surrounded by green meadows, views, and a lot of people.

From Blausee, follow the trail, which climbs over a rocky ridge at an elevation of 2250 meters. For the best long-distance views, cross the ridge and detour upward on any trail that follows the ridge line or along the hillside; for close-up views of the ice, there is a trail that leads to the edge of the glacier. Keep a lookout for chamois. A herd of them lives on the upper ridge.

To return to the valley, follow any trail that heads down from the ridgetop toward Rieder Furka, then catch the cable car at Riederalp, 14 km, elevation 1909 meters, to Morel, where you can take a train back to Fiesch or head down the valley to Brig.

35   MÄSSERSEE

Round trip 5 km, 3 miles
Hiking time 3½ hours
High point 2137 meters, 7009 feet

Elevation gain 736 meters,
2414 feet
Maps: Nufenpass 265,
V. Antigorio 275

We were so attracted by the village of Ernen located just across the way from Fiesch (see Hike No. 34) that we spontaneously decided to explore this little-known area and the hikes it had to offer. After a walk through the twisted streets of town, where the heavy wood chalets are marvelously colored by flowers and the small, quaint gardens full of vegetables and flowers as well, we continued up the valley to the village of Binn, which also proved to be very picturesque, just like in Swiss calendars, only these chalets had *real* people living in them! The campground, ½ km farther up the valley, was laid out along the Binna River and had excellent facilities and promising views. By the way, if you do not have access to an automobile, there are six post buses per day to Binn from Brig, 27 glorious km.

The next day we took a short hike up to the Mässersee. We walked ½ km up the macadam road from the campground in an easterly direction, to a shop that sold jewelry and mountain stones, and asked for directions. With our broken German and a lot of gestures, we learned that there was a pyrite mine up the dirt road. We continued on the road and wound around a waterfall to the quarry where there were half a dozen amateur geologists chipping away very seriously. But we were hikers, not miners, and a few meters farther on there was a junction with a trail heading left marked "BERGWEG." So we went up the mountain trail. The trail steepened as it wound through a rich forest, emerging from time to time into a clearing where there were ruins of old stone huts. In bad weather, these could provide shelter. After 1¼ hours on good but unmarked trail we emerged onto a plateau where there were clear trail signs indicating the Mässersee/Geisspfaesee. We walked through blueberries and flowers,

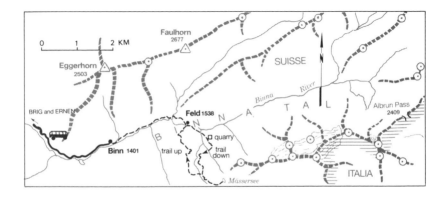

Other trail users, below Mässersee (photo by Suzy Edwards)

crossed the stream two times, and emerged at 2137 meters onto a high plateau completely surrounded by high stone cliffs. The site was impressive, but the lake was barely a pond. Two years of little rain or snow had practically dried it up. However, the site was spectacular: a cirque with the pond in the middle looking toward the Rhone Valley with a slew of glaciers and Swiss villages standing out from the forests. We got a good view of where we had been the day before and after studying the map we realized we were very close to the Italian border.

To return, we followed the Bergweg, crossed a rushing stream, and zigzagged through the forest and past a herd of cows to the road. Back in camp we studied the map and realized that there was a long and potentially exciting hike to be made up the Binna Valley, through the Albrun Pass into the Italian lake country high above the city of Locarno. We're looking forward to that.

36   OESCHINENSEE

Round trip 10 km, 6 miles
Hiking time 4 hours
High point 1767 meters, 5796 feet

Elevation gain 567 meters,
    1860 feet
Map: Berner Oberland 5004

Almost every Swiss calendar contains a picture of the Oeschinensee. This lake is a lovely place and our aim was to get up there and try to take a picture as good or better than the ones in the calendars. But the day we tried to get up there the morning was wet and foggy, we were slow getting out of the tents, and there was doubt we would see anything of the lake or of the peaks that are reflected in it.

We were also worried that the crowds of people who go up to the Oeschinensee every day would make a good picture impossible. Most of them were transported by a chairlift to within 15 minutes of the summit. The sense of solitude we associate, no doubt selfishly, with the mountains would inevitably be lost, so we decided to try to reach the Gasthaus Unter Bergli, a small hotel where it was said the views were more grandiose, and with fewer people to interrupt them.

The hike starts in the town of Kandersteg, reached by train or road from Brig to the south and Spiez to the north. The trail toward the lake is well marked from both the railroad station and the highway. We picked it up just before the entrance to the Rendezvous Campground. From there you follow the direction for Grünenwald and you rise through the forest along the river. This way up is a bit longer than taking the jeep road that runs by the chairlift, and definitely longer than taking the chairlift up and traversing across to meet the road rising from the valley. Starting on the left side of the river, the macadam road peters out after the electric generator plant, becomes a dirt road, and finally heads left into the woods. The switchbacks steepen, then the trail levels out and crosses a brook on the left. On the way up, you can't help but notice a

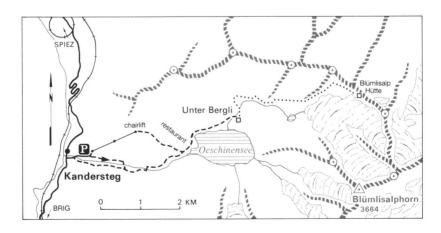

Fishing in Oeschinensee

150-foot-long stream of water that gushes dramatically out of a notch across the valley. When the trail runs perpendicularly into the road, you take the road to the left and eventually you arrive at Oeschinensee, 1578 meters.

The fog had been with us all along and our spirits were low. But you could feel the sun penetrating the blanket layer hiding the beauty we knew was present. Suddenly, there was a break in the clouds; the sun danced in and out, the wind came up, and—a hiker's dream—the lake was swept clear and the peaks burst forth. Rock walls rose up almost vertically 1000 feet high to end in glaciers and snow-white ridges. It was even better than the photographs we had seen. Out came the cameras.

We hiked the shores of the lake for the best angles and, to satiate our appetites even more, we went on. From the restaurant at the outlet of the lake we picked up the trail marked "GASTHAUS UNTER BERGLI," which climbed a ledge on the north side of the lake and after 5 km arrived at the guest house, 1767 meters.

37 WENGEN

One way 12 km, 7½ miles	Elevation loss 1434 meters,
Hiking time 3 hours	4704 feet
High point 2229 meters, 7311 feet	Map: Berner Oberland 5004 or
Elevation gain 200 meters, 656 feet	Interlaken 254

We have returned many times to do this hike because it is one of our Swiss favorites. The cog railroad takes you to the base of the Eiger, where you walk an easy trail along a green ridge with views of Grindelwald and the Wetterhorn, and then drop down to Wengen and see Lauterbrunnen Valley—a textbook example of a U-shaped glacier-carved valley.

From Interlaken, go by train or car to the town of Lauterbrunnen and take the cog railroad to Kleine Scheidegg, elevation 2061 meters. From Kleine Scheidegg you can see the famous north face of the Eiger. If any climbers are on the face, and there often are, their progress can be followed by telescope. From Kleine Scheidegg the railroad tunnels up inside the Eiger to the Jungfraujoch, where there is a superb viewpoint with fantastic views of the Aletsch Glacier, the longest glacier in the Alps (see Hike No. 34). Even though there is no place to hike from there and the train trip is very expensive, it is well worth every Swiss franc.

Back down at the Kleine Scheidegg station, head north along a prominent ridge with views of Grindelwald, farms, and mountains. At 4 km you reach the Männlichen Hotel at 2229 meters, the high point of this hike. From there the trail drops over the west side of the ridge, crosses under the wires of a cable car, and descends, at times very steeply, toward the alpine town of Wengen and views into the Lauterbrunnen Valley. As the trail levels out and approaches the farmlands above Wengen, there are many branching paths and service roads. The way is well marked and the distance to town is about 8 km. The towns of Wengen

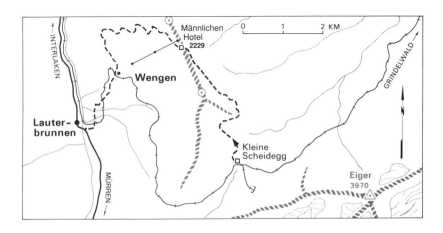

and Zermatt are among nineteen tourist areas in Switzerland where automobiles are prohibited.

For the best views of the Lauterbrunnen Valley, detour on any likely looking right-hand trail where a broad shoulder gives a straight look up the valley. When you are satisfied with the view, head back to Wengen, and, at the railroad station, pick up the trail down to Lauterbrunnen, 12 km from Kleine Scheidegg.

Queen of the cow herd returning home from summer pasture

38 OBERHORNSEE

Round trip 16 km, 10 miles
Hiking time 4 hours up, 3 hours
down
High point 2065 meters, 6773 feet
Elevation gain 1155 meters,
3788 feet
Map: Berner Oberland 5004

Chamois at Obersteinberg

Because of its isolation and very limited development, this is one of the most rewarding hikes in the Lauterbrunnen Valley, not far from Interlaken. Traffic in the valley ends at the hamlet of Stechelberg, elevation 910 meters. From there, up the valley by foot, there are no cable cars, waterworks, or manicured ski slopes to mar the views. The farms and mountain hotels, perched on slopes and rock pinnacles, are still on the simple side, and man's presence has left few permanent scars. On the way up to this lake, you hike through a cool forest and green meadows where the chamois graze, past rushing torrents and waterfalls.

Although this is a fine jaunt in cloudy weather when the colors are subtle, the chamois less timid, and the people fewer, the hike becomes sensational in fine weather when the mountains are seen against a back-

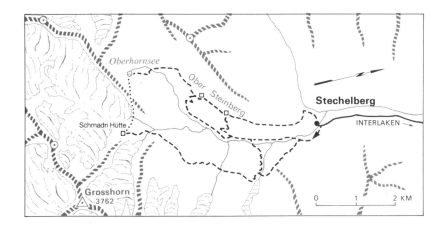

Oberhornsee

drop of clear blue sky, and the glacier-covered summits of the Jungfrau, Breithorn, and the bare cliffs of the Ellstabhorn are all visible. From Interlaken there are many buses that service the Lauterbrunnen Valley. Stechelberg is the last stop. At the hamlet's south end is a trail wide enough for a tractor that starts up the left (east) side of the valley. At ¾ km, it crosses the Weisse Lutschine River and then heads steeply up the right side of the valley. At 2 km, the trail passes a small hotel at Trachsel-lauenen, the end of the tractor route. At 2½ km, the trail forks. Both routes go upvalley: the left fork follows the torrent and then forks again with a possible side trip to a large waterfall; the right fork is in better condition and offers better views. We went right and came down the left trail.

The right-hand trail switchbacks steeply up to alpine meadows that offer views of the valley and mountains. At 4½ km, elevation 1685 meters, you reach a hotel at Obersteinberg and then contour to a second hotel at 5 km. Fine views. Continuing on, the trail pretty much follows the contours of the meadows, with a few ups and downs, until it crosses a stream. Then it steepens and switchbacks up a rocky promontory a short distance from the Oberhornsee, a small blue-green lake with mountains reflecting in it at 8 km, 2065 meters.

We ran into a herd of chamois early in the morning. Their brown color, so hard to pick out in the woods, makes them far more visible when they are grazing in green meadows. Skittish and quick, they are wary of humans and if you are upwind and they sense your presence, they will dash for the nearest wood.

To vary your descent, from Oberhornsee follow a paint-marked trail east to the Schmadri Hütte, elevation 2263 meters, and return on the opposite side of the valley; or you can backtrack past the hotels, stay high, and catch a trail marked "MÜRREN" and at Schwendi, 1155 meters, drop down to Stechelberg.

39   FAULHORN

One way 15 km, 9½ miles   Elevation gain 700 meters,
Hiking time 6 hours   2296 feet
High point 2600 meters, 8528 feet   Map: Berner Oberland 5004

The first time we attempted this hike we were engulfed in clouds most of
the way and were tantalized by fleeting glimpses of the beautiful sights.
So we hiked it again on a clear day.

The hike follows a high ridge with the low hills of northern Switzerland on one side and, on the south side, the frightening north face of the
Eiger and the glacier-clad mountains of the Bernese Oberland. As you
walk along the ridge, you can look down more than 2000 meters and see
sailboats on the Brienzer See and, in the valley on the south side, tiny
villages snuggled beneath the hills. These views are so dramatic that we
are convinced that, because of the views that are its principal attraction,
this is one hike that should only be attempted on a clear day. Besides,
even though the main and side trails are well marked, the route crosses
some rock gullies, and snow may still be present even in August. So it is
better to see where you are going.

By using uphill transportation, you can make this a round trip. From
Interlaken travel to Wilderswil, and from there take the cog railroad to
Schynige Platte, elevation 2067 meters. At the railroad station, find the
trail marked "FAULHORN." It contours slightly up on the south side of the
ridge. At just over 2 km, you reach a high point; then a gentle slope
downward brings you to a short series of switchbacks leading up to a
2067-meter-high pass at 4 km. Now the trail climbs as it contours a hillside high above the Sagistalsee, a small lake with two farms on its
shores. Then it turns a corner and passes Weber Hütte, a small restaurant. Beyond the restaurant, the trail steepens slightly, climbing a barren ridge, and, at 9 km, elevation 2660 meters, it goes a few meters below

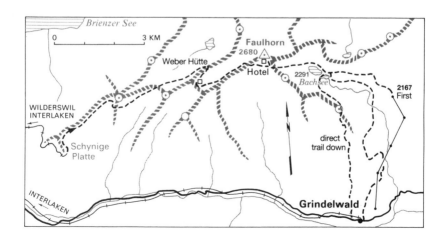

The Faulhorn

a large hotel on top of a promontory called the Faulhorn. From here you will have the best view down to Brienzer See to the north and the Jungfrau Range to the south.

From the hotel, the trail then descends to the Bachsee, a beautiful lake and pond surrounded by green hills. There, either take a lower trail marked "GRINDELWALD," losing some 1200 meters (a healthy drop and a good 2- to 3-hour walk), or from Bachsee remain on the upper trail, which takes you to the top terminal of the First chairlift at 15 km. A word of warning: Before starting out on this hike, at the Wilderswil station or at the Grindelwald tourist office (telephone 036 53 12 12) find out if the First chairlift is operating and when it closes in the evening. Then, if you decide to take the lift down, be sure to leave sufficient time from the Bachsee to the top terminal of the lift; otherwise you may have to walk down about 7 km and 1000 vertical meters to Grindelwald, from where you catch the train back to Wilderswil.

40 GROßE SCHEIDEGG

One way 15 km, 9½ miles	**Elevation gain 100 meters, 328 feet**
Hiking time 1½ hours up,	**Elevation loss 905 meters,**
2½ hours down	**2968 feet**
High point 3000 meters, 9840 feet	**Map: Berner Oberland 5004**

Only in a few areas in the Alps—Austria's Großglockner, France's Chamonix, and Switzerland's Zermatt and Grindelwald—can you so easily gain altitude and experience a deep surge of emotion. Views are breathtaking and you stand in awe at the tremendous power, beauty, and variety of the mountains. Going up to Große Scheidegg via a high mountain pass and tiny Hornseeli Lake under the towering north side of the Wetterhorn (the beautiful mountain that dominates the resort city of Grindelwald) is an example of just such a hike.

Many high-altitude farms are found along the trail, and civilization has left its impression here in other ways. While private automobiles are barred, the trip to Große Scheidegg can be made entirely by motor bus; or most of the elevation can be gained by use of the First chairlift. Of course, it is feasible to walk both ways. There is much to see and many branching roads and trails, so that it is possible to return by a different route than you came by. However, for a day hike, we had to make a compromise and it was with some chagrin that we rode the chairlift up, hiked around, and walked back down.

From Grindelwald, elevation 1057 meters, follow the signs to the First chairlift. There are three sections to the lift and a fourth is planned; but just remain on it until it reaches the top station at an elevation of 2167 meters. From there take the trail headed east (right). With many ups and downs, you walk along the hillside to Oberläger, a small cluster of farm buildings. Continue on and at 3½ km you reach a fork. The right trail follows the divide down and at 5 km arrives at Große Scheidegg;

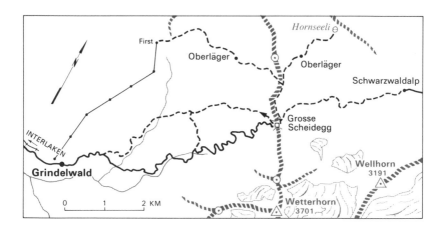

Hornseeli and cloud-covered Wetterhorn

but, for the time being, stay on the left trail and hike to the second farm-house cluster that is also called Oberläger.

To reach Hornseeli Lake, which is higher up, continue on, cross the stream, and soon reach a junction. Stay on the left trail for a short distance, and then leave it and make your way uphill to the right onto a well-trod path that climbs steeply to the lake.

To return, retrace your steps to the intersection with the main trail going down to the pass and hotel-restaurant at Große Scheidegg. From there, either follow the paved road 10 km back to Grindelwald, or follow the trail that can be seen going down a green ridge. The trail is a lot steeper than the road, but easily saves a kilometer of relatively uninteresting hiking. If you have no reason to return to Grindelwald, you can follow the service road eastward from Große Scheidegg down to Schwarzwaldalp and catch the bus back to Interlaken via Meiringen. Although buses are frequent, be sure to check schedules in advance.

41 THE GRINDELWALD GLACIER CIRQUE

Round trip 10 km, 6¼ miles
Hiking time 6 to 7 hours
High point 1807 meters, 5927 feet

Elevation gain 821 meters,
2693 feet
Map: Berner Oberland 5004

Between the mighty Eiger, 3970 meters, and the 4078-meter-high Schreckhorn lies a magnificent glacial cirque that funnels down toward Grindelwald. In not many other areas in the Alps are the forces of nature so concentrated, evident, and accessible to view: the huge Fiescher Glacier comes out of the east face of the Eiger, while from the west at least three smaller forceful glaciers pour out of the Schreckhorn, Lauteraarhorn, and Nässihorn to form the upper and lower Eismeer glaciers, until finally everything is compressed into the Grindelwald Glacier, held to its banks by high cliffs. All of these frozen waterfalls form mountains of seracs—huge pillars and blocks of ice—as the pressures of gravity, wind, rain, and continual changes in temperature work for and against each other. Ice avalanches and ice blocks come roaring down onto the glaciers;

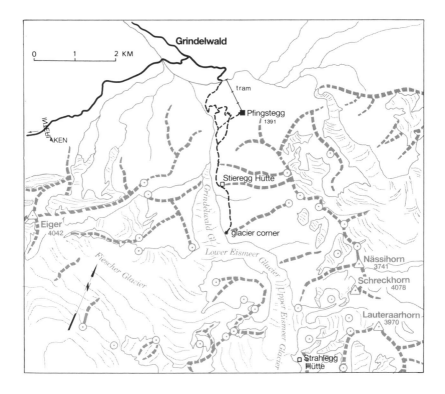

The Grindelwald Glacier Cirque

rocks plummet down the cliffs, while far below the ice the swirling waters combine and issue, finally, as a roaring river. There isn't a better place to see all of this than from a safe viewpoint above the Stieregg Hütte.

You can save an hour's hiking through meadows and woods by taking the Pfingstegg tram from Grindelwald to the top station at 1391 meters. From there, pick up the trail to the Stieregg mountain restaurant. The trail dips, goes through two gates, and swings around a buttress. While you can, enjoy the calm views of Grindelwald below; dramatic views are in store up ahead. A short, steep climb up a ramp together with side views of the Eiger's north face will get your heartbeat into rhythm. Ten minutes out, with cows, sheep, and goats all about, the trail coming up from Grindelwald arrives from the right. On the way down, this is the trail you take to Marmorbruch, 25 minutes, and to the Gletscherschlucht, 1 hour. The last 15 minutes of the trail before you reach the hut has been blasted out of the side of the cliff, and at places your only protection on this catwalk is a railing that is anchored to the rock. Walk carefully.

From the restaurant the boulder-strewn trail is marked with cairns and red paint slashes, but we lost them at one point. Finally, you arrive at what we nicknamed "Glacier Corner"—a splendid viewpoint about 2 hours from the Strahlegg hut, 2688 meters, which is practically down on the glacier itself.

The way to Grindelwald is a back track past the Stieregg hut where, by the way, you can also rent a room for the night. You continue down the catwalk trail and pick up the valley route (now taking off to your left) that you passed on the way up.

Another extraordinary feature of this hike is the many different kinds of stone—marble, gneiss, slate, and limestone—often polished by glacial movement, that can be spotted along the trails and on the cliffs—a veritable geologist's paradise.

42 ALBERT HEIM HÜTTE TO ANDERMATT

One way 15 km, 9½ miles	**Elevation gain 520 meters,**
Hiking time 6 to 7 hours	**1706 feet**
High point 2541 meters, 8334 feet	**Maps: Sustenpass 255;**
	Urseren 1231, 1:25,000

This hike combines the fun of an easy climb to a pleasant mountain cabin, where you can stay overnight, and a long sun-soaked traverse across the flanks of the mountains to your starting point. First you walk around a steep ridge with views of the glacier-clad Galenstock and the exciting rock spires of the Winterstock. Next, you traverse a good part of the valley above the Furka River where, at more than 3000 meters, you

Albert Heim Hütte and the Winterstock

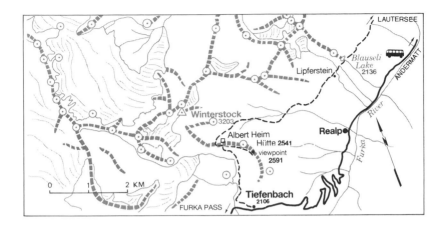

are almost guaranteed to find flowers such as alpine rose, soldanella, edelweiss, and many other varieties.

There is no need for an automobile on this trip. From Andermatt, catch the post bus, which runs three times daily in summer, to the tiny village of Tiefenbach, located 2106 meters high on a steep mountain slope on the east side of the Furka Pass. From the village, follow the new road approximately 1 km up to what was once a parking lot. The trailhead is marked with a red slash on a white background. At about 1½ km the new trail joins an old trail coming up from the Furka Pass road and at 2 km you reach Albert Heim Hütte, elevation 2541 meters. On the comfortable balcony of this hut we treated ourselves to a cup of tea and a piece of Swiss pastry, and to work it off took a very pleasant side trip up a south path along a ridgetop to a 2591-meter-high viewpoint. There were fine views of the Gotthard Massif and the nearby Grison and Tessin Alps. From there we returned to the hut and picked up a trail heading north. After a few hundred meters the trail turns in an easterly direction toward Andermatt. Since there are several turnoffs to villages in the valley, it is a good idea to keep your contour map handy for consultation. In general, the traversing trail heads east to Lipferstein, to Blauseeli Lake at 2136 meters, past the Luterseeli lakes, by the military camp at Rossmettlen at 2091 meters, and then, depending on which of the many trails you decide to return on, begins the long downhill to Andermatt, elevation 1439 meters.

43   THREE MOUNTAIN HUTS

Round trip 15 km, 9½ miles
Hiking time 5 hours up,
   3½ hours down
High point 2350 meters, 7708 feet

Elevation gain 1663 meters,
   5455 feet
Map: Sustenpass 255 or
   Urseren 1231

This hike provides three different choices: The first, 2½ km from the start, is the Bergsee Hütte, located next to an alpine tarn with sweeping views. It's an easy, rewarding jaunt. Second is the Damma Hütte, located on the other side of the Chelen Valley 3 hours away. And third is the interesting climb to the Chelenalp Hütte. If you visit all three huts—and it's worth it—be prepared for a long day of walking and climbing (1663 meters vertical).

Take the post bus or drive north from Andermatt to the town of Göschenen. From there you travel 10 km up a lovely valley on a narrow road with winding curves almost 700 meters higher up to Göscheneralp. Park in the lot near the huge earth dam behind which is the Göscheneralpsee. Many people are content with an easy 4-hour walking tour around the artificial lake, which is dominated by the Dammastock-kwette mountain. But the three-hut trail, with much more varied views, begins at the upper end of the parking lot. The trail climbs in a series of short switchbacks to two small tarns, levels off, and in 1 km reaches a junction with the trail to the Bergsee Hütte, 300 vertical meters higher up and about 2 km farther on. Located near a small lake, it's a lovely spot and the steep climb up to the hut is well worth the effort.

After visiting that hut, you come down the same trail and at about 1800 meters you reach the junction. Turn right and descend first gently and then steeply to the head of the reservoir, losing virtually all the elevation you gained. At 2½ km, at the edge of the torrent called Chelen-reuss, the trail forks. The left fork crosses the torrent and climbs steeply

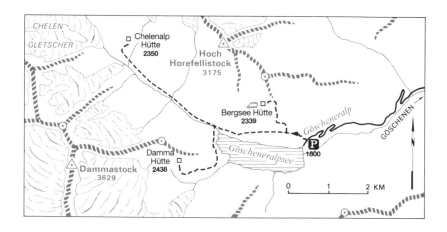

Chelenreuss (river)

to the Damma Hütte, elevation 2438 meters. Visit that one as well and when you descend to pick up the trail to the Chelenalp Hütte, stay on the right side of the stream. In places it dashes over rocks; elsewhere it meanders lazily along the valley, which has a classic U-shape formed by ancient glaciers; in season the valley floor is covered with flowers.

At about 6½ km, near the rubble-covered snout of the Chelen Glacier, the trail, which has been slowly climbing, leaves the valley floor for the Chelenalp Hütte, 200 steep meters up. From the hut's balcony you are now able to compare the views with those of the other two huts. Spread before you are glaciers, alpine pastures, roaring torrents, and the now-distant reservoir.

44 ALTEINSEE

Round trip 8 km, 5 miles
Hiking time 4½ hours
High point 2251 meters, 7383 feet

Elevation gain 640 meters,
 2099 feet
Maps: Bergün 258, Prattigau 248

If you happen to be in Davos and you want to go to Arosa (or vice versa), which is just on the other side of the mountains, it's a good 3-hour drive via Chur on a narrow, winding road; by post bus, with changes, it is probably 5 to 6 hours. So a hike over the mountains is worth consideration. It might take you 5 hours, but it's a lot healthier, certainly cheaper, and, from our point of view, far more interesting than motorized tourism. We discovered this alternative too late, but next time around that's the way we will go.

If you spend the night in Arosa, which caters to a lot of skiers in winter and old folks in summer, the climb to Altein Lake is a better hike than you might think. However, locating the trailhead in this hilly city is not easy. From the Esso station at the entrance to town, take the Alteinstrasse to Alteinplatz where you pick up Neubachstrasse. At the signs bear right down to the water treatment plant at the end of the road, 1610 meters. If you have come by train, walk around either side of Obersee, the lake directly in front of the station, to the Esso station.

From the parking lot, follow a service road in front of the water treatment plant. This soon becomes a wide trail that climbs through blueberry bushes and arolla pines along the Wälschtobelbach River. Markings are red slashes on a white background. At 1½ km, 1643 meters, you cross a wooden bridge; shortly thereafter you cross the Alteinbach on another bridge. The trail steepens noticeably and switchbacks up, alternating between a scrub forest and a rock slide. Near the top of the slide is a junction. Since the directional sign is often displaced by avalanches, note that the left fork makes a worthwhile detour to an over-

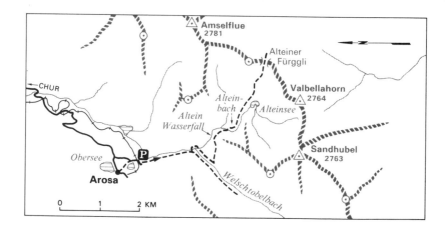

Altein Waterfall

look from where you can observe the beautiful Altein Waterfall. The right fork switchbacks up a steep terrace, and 3 km farther on it reaches open meadows. The red slashes are prominent here and the trail boulder-hops Altein stream and continues up in sight of two more waterfalls. At 4 km, elevation 2251 meters, it passes a few meters above the crescent-shaped Alteinsee. This lake is the center of a kilometer-wide meadow with meandering bubbling brooks worthy of Wordsworth. There are ridges to explore and meadows to roam in, and it's a marvelous place to stretch out in and relax. Two small wooden cabins are above the lake, one of which has a solar panel to provide current for the electric cattle fence, and the other has crude benches and tables meant, no doubt, for tired hikers.

From the lake, the trail continues another 2 km to Alteiner Fürggli pass at 2491 meters, where a sketchy trail leads to the 2764-meter summit of Valbellahorn Mountain, which rises directly behind the lake. To return to Arosa, retrace your steps.

45 FUORCLA DA GRIALETSCH

Round trip 8 km, 5 miles
Hiking time 4 hours
High point 2537 meters, 8321 feet

Elevation gain 537 meters,
1761 feet
Map: Wanderkarte Davos or
Bergün 258

This is an ideal family hike or afternoon jaunt to a small lake, mountain views, and a mountain hut. From early July, you will find acres and acres of alpine rose—rhododendron bushes with red-pink blossoms. The naturalness of the scenery is in stark contrast to the cement city of Davos that you have left behind—the skyscrapers, condominiums, traffic, and

Grialetsch Hütte

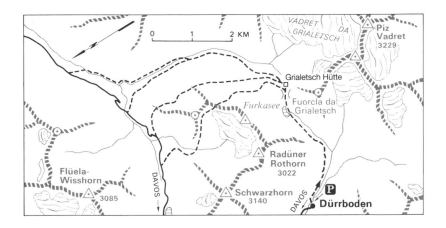

bustling activity reminiscent of Los Angeles. With relief, one travels up the narrow road to near the head of the Dischma Valley to the parking-lot trailhead at Dürrboden, 13 km.

Happily, there are now four buses a day from Davos to the parking lot and the new cafeteria-restaurant where hot and cold meals are served, 2007 meters. It's amazing how the big buses maneuver on the one-lane, windy road. You skirt the golf course, turn right at the road marked "DISCHMA" (south), and follow the Dischmabach stream past the log huts and houses around which the cows are grazing and the ducks paddling happily in the ponds. You can also walk the excellent trail all the way from Davos. This will give you ample time to enjoy the old farm buildings and flowers; besides, there are benches to sit on and several restaurants, hotels, and cafés along the way should you wish to interrupt the hike.

The trail from the parking lot is not terribly well marked and the hiking is made bothersome by cobblestone, but there is little chance of getting lost. When the trail forks, keep left. Unexpectedly, at about the halfway point, the trail becomes well graded and the hiking is much easier. At approximately 3½ km the trail passes Furkasee, a shallow tarn, and at 4 km reaches Fuorcla da Grialetsch, a pass 2537 meters high. Hike a few meters farther to the Grialetsch hut and a commanding view of the Vadret da Grialetsch, a wide glacier.

At the pass the trail divides into three rough tracks to the Flüelapass road; all are marked with red and white paint. From the road there are frequent buses, and you can return to Davos from there.

For ramblings around the hut and better views, hike the uppermost of the three trails to a high shoulder on the side of Piz Radont; or follow a climber's path that rises to a shoulder of Piz Grialetsch and goes across the top of a moraine to the edge of Grialetsch Glacier.

We were the first people to leave the parking lot at 5:00 in the morning. We hadn't gone more than 500 meters when two chamois came charging down the mountainside. They crossed the trail about 100 meters ahead of us, made a big loop, crossed 100 meters behind us, and, still running full tilt, disappeared up the mountainside.

46 VAL MULIX

Round trip 11 km, 7 miles
Hiking time 4 hours
High point 2622 meters, 8600 feet

Elevation gain 833 meters,
2732 feet
Map: Bergün 258

Many trails in the Alps lead to more impressive views, but Val Mulix is uncrowded and, at least on the rainy day we were there, it offered us a chance to enjoy the solitude of dripping forests, humid alpine meadows, and a small lake that is frozen much of the year. It was a wet day but not so bad that we couldn't get something wonderful out of it.

On the highway between Zernez and Pontresina, the Albula Pass road takes off from the hamlet of La Punt. After the pass, which is full of high-tension wires and rock slides, you come to a tiny group of houses in an area called Naz. Park your car as far off the road as possible, or drive it through the narrow tunnel and park higher up among the farmhouses. Most of these houses have been restored and, with a couple of exceptions, are secondary residences. It's a pretty little spot, even in the fog and rain, and you would not at all be surprised to see a deer or two grazing peacefully.

From the uppermost farmhouse the trailhead can be found at 1789 meters. The trail enters the forest, crosses a turbulent stream via a wooden bridge, and climbs up steeply for about 1½ km to a fork. The well-worn right trail heads up to Pass d'Ela. Take the lesser-used left path, which follows the Mulix River up the Val Mulix. The trail levels a bit and at times becomes indistinct as it crosses a marshy alpine pasture; but even if you lose it, the only route is up the valley. About 800 meters from the fork you pass a farm hut, and the trail steepens. At about 4 km, the valley and trail make an abrupt right turn and both end at Lake Negr, elevation 2622 meters, at 5½ km.

Naz is also the starting point for a full-day or overnight hike, much of

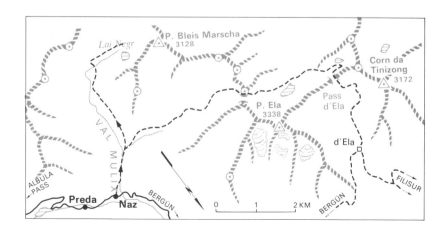

Decorated facade of a house in Bergün (photo by Suzy Edwards)

which is above timberline. Take the same trail to the fork, but instead of going left, follow the steep trail to the right, which switches back and forth through the woods to timberline and a small restaurant. Continue steadily up through green meadows and boulder slopes to the Pass d'Ela at 2725 meters. From there the trail, marked by cairns and painted stripes, descends gradually for another 3 km to the Swiss Mountain Club's d'Ela hut at 2252 meters. You can stay overnight there or continue down 7 km to either Bergün or Filisur. From Naz it is a good 5½ hours to the pass and another 4 hours to Filisur.

47   ALP GRIMMELS
(Swiss National Park)

Loop trip 7 km, 4¼ miles   **Elevation gain 300 meters, 984 feet**
Hiking time 2½ hours   **Map: Ofenpass 259**
High point 2100 meters, 6888 feet

The main features of this forest hike in the Swiss National Park are the
many red deer and marmots that the hiker has a good chance of seeing.
It's also a good introduction to the way the Swiss manage the rich natural resources in the park.

Red deer

In most countries, national parks are formed to protect some unique feature such as scenery or wildlife. If scenery were the only criterion, almost all of Switzerland would qualify as a national park. In comparison to the rest of the Alps, the mountains in the Swiss National Park are relatively tame. However, as you will learn at the visitor center on the outskirts of Zernez (exhibits and audiovisual materials are shown), the park is a large nature preserve where flowers are not picked by man or eaten by cows, and animals are never hunted. Man is the intruder and must abide by certain *very* strict rules. Hikers are allowed on park trails, but they must stay on them. A tired hiker may rest alongside the trail, but must not wander too far off toward a stream or shade tree. Lunch stops are permitted only at designated locations and their limits are marked with stakes. No camping is allowed—anywhere, anytime.

Daybreak and dusk are the best times to see the red deer. At that time of day the meadows are heavily grazed. But during the heat of day, the deer retreat to the woods, chewing their cuds. In certain areas ibex can be seen. In this protected setting, they are less wary of humans and you may find them grazing quietly on the upper cliffs. Marmots love heat and once the sun comes up you can see them feeding and frolicking in the meadows, never very far from their burrows. As you approach, they may let out a strident cry—their way of letting other marmots in the area know that there is danger approaching.

From Zernez, travel the Ofenpass road southeast toward Italy for 9 km to Park Place No. 2, elevation 1800 meters. The unmarked trailhead is on the uphill side of the highway. In ½ km, you reach a junction. Keep straight ahead. The trail climbs very steeply, gaining 200 meters. It then levels off and traverses a steep mountainside to a wooded pass at 2100 meters. Beyond the pass, the trail descends slightly to Alp Grimmels and a rest area (no water available), elevation 2000 meters, at 2½ km. From there continue on to a junction in 3¼ km, then keep left and descend a dry valley. At 6 km, you return to the highway at Park Place No. 1 and are only 1 km from your starting point.

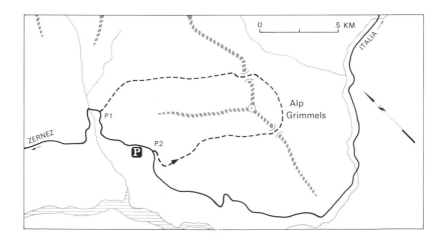

48   ALP TRUPCHUN
(Swiss National Park)

Round trip 12 km, 7½ miles
Hiking time 4 hours
High point 2040 meters, 6691 feet

Elevation gain 380 meters,
1246 feet
Map: Wanderkarte Oberengadin-
Bernina or Ofenpass 259

Flowers, animals, and rich vegetation are what you will find in abundance in the Alp Trupchun area of the Swiss National Park. Red deer, steinbok (ibex), chamois, and marmots are the commonest animals. In May and early June, the animals are frequently seen along the valley bottom trail; but as the snow melts they move higher up, and in summer they are often just tiny dots on a distant mountainside. It's a good idea to carry binoculars, and some animal watchers set up powerful telescopes on tripods in meadows and along the trails. The trails are sufficient attraction; but to see the animals in their natural setting surrounded by green meadows and colorful flowers makes hiking in the park very special.

From the town of S-chanf in the Inn Valley, walk or drive 2 km on the road marked either "VARUSCH" or "NATIONAL PARK" to the road's end, elevation 1660 meters. From there, follow a jeep trail ½ km, cross Ova da Varusch (a stream), and attain the rustic Varusch hut after 1½ km. The jeep road ends at the hut, where there is a confusion of trails. You can either stay at the stream level or climb up into the forest as we did. From there, through the larch and arolla pine, you have good views of the riverbed below and the snow-studded mountains of Val Trupchun up ahead. In 1¾ km, the trail enters the national park, which is clearly marked with a big sign. The trail climbs steadily. We saw a lot of gentian and thistle flowers as soon as the trees gave way to the grass meadows of Alp Trupchun. We spent an hour or so watching the marmots eating and

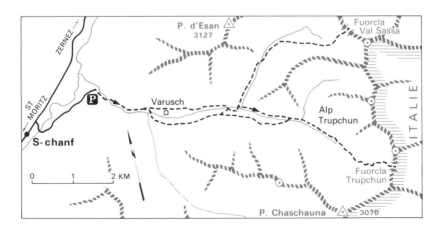

Alp Trupchun (photo by Suzy Edwards)

chasing around the meadows. Beside the junction of the valley bottom trail and the high trail, you find the first designated rest area. A second one is well up in the meadow beside an old farmhouse now used by park rangers.

Early morning and evening, when the animals are feeding, are the best times of day to observe them. During the heat of the day they often lie down and are hard to spot. Herds of twenty to fifty red deer feed on the open slopes, while the steinbok, almost as if to tempt tourists' cameras, often appear as silhouettes along the ridge lines. Deer, chamois, and steinbok move around a great deal, and if you don't see them in the lower meadows, sometimes it is worthwhile to climb higher. Rangers in the park, who know the animals' habits best, can often give good advice about where to find them.

On the return, we stayed low along the valley bottom trail back to the road.

49 FUORCLA VAL SASSA
(Swiss National Park)

One way 24 km, 15 miles
Hiking time 1½ days
High point 2857 meters, 9731 feet

Elevation gain 1425 meters,
4674 feet
Map: Ofenpass 259

We are accustomed to traveling around national parks, pitching our tent, and enjoying the late-evening and early-morning views of the animals and birds. That, however, is not possible in the Swiss National Park, mainly because the park, like Switzerland itself, is small and extremely popular. Tourists visit from all over the world, entire schools come to study nature "in the raw," and there just isn't enough space to accommodate campgrounds and still maintain the natural habitat of the park, which is devoted to protecting the flora and fauna.

For that reason, any overnight hikes like this one from S-chanf to Zernez (or vice versa) require an overnight stop. And the only place to stay in the park is at the Chamanna Cluozza, a rustic mountain inn. It's a long walk, but you are sure to see many animals along the way.

The trail traverses a high, barren pass with a view of the Piz Quattervals, the highest peak in the park. From S-chanf follow the directions for the Val Trupchun (Hike No. 48). Pass the Varusch hut and enter the park, continuing upstream 3 km to an intersection. The right fork follows Trupchun stream to Val Trupchun. Take the left fork and immediately cross Muschauns stream on a wooden bridge. The trail, rather sketchy at times, crosses the stream again at 4 km and then climbs steeply to another crossing. Finally at 9 km it reaches Fuorcla Val Sassa, a 2857-meter-high pass. On the far side of the pass the route is marked

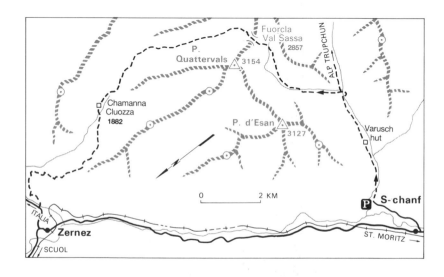

Trail bridge over the Muschauns (river)

by paint. It goes over scree and snow patches, making it difficult to follow in poor weather. Eventually, the trail enters the forest, and at 15 km from the trailhead it reaches the Chamanna Cluozza inn, elevation 1882 meters.

The next day, continue on the same trail, dropping 80 meters to a stream crossing; then contour and climb 280 meters to a ridge overlooking the Inn Valley. From here the trail descends in a series of switchbacks to farm fields. The trail eventually becomes a farm road, crosses the Spol River, and at 24 km reaches the Ofenpass highway about 1 km from Zernez. You can return to S-chanf by train or bus.

Chamois at the base of Tschierva Glacier

50 TSCHIERVA HÜTTE

Round trip 25 km, 15½ miles
Hiking time 4 hours up,
   3 hours down
High point 2573 meters, 8439 feet

Elevation gain 799 meters,
   2620 feet
Map: Julier Pass 268 or
   Oberengadin, 1:60,000

A hike up the Roseg River Valley to the Tschierva Hütte is very worthwhile because of its views. Also, it is one of the best places in the Grisons region to see marmots and chamois—the elusive mountain antelope.

The trail starts near the railroad station in Pontresina, 1774 meters.

Walk toward town for about 100 meters; next to the bridge over the Roseg River is a sign marked "HOTEL ROSEG." From there, you can either walk up the right side of the valley, on a dirt road used only by horse carriages and an occasional delivery truck, or on the left side of the river on a very busy footpath. Either way is easy, with a vertical climb of only 200 meters for 7 km.

Just before reaching the Hotel Roseg, close to where the road crosses the river, the Tschierva Hütte trail can be found on the left bank. The trail follows the flat, wide valley for another kilometer and then starts up in earnest. As the trail climbs, the views unfold: first the Roseg Glacier, then the Tschierva Glacier dominated by Piz Roseg. Within sight of the hut, the trail follows a gully between the lateral moraine and the hillside. At one point you can climb onto the moraine itself. The view is definitely better up there, but the moraine is sloughing away and the trail makes several detours. It is best to continue in the gully, even though you may be obliged to cross patches of snow.

The Tschierva Hütte, perched at 2573 meters, is operated by the Swiss Alpine Club and offers meals and dormitory accommodations on a first-come, first-served basis. For even better views of the mountains and the Piz Bernina, it is worthwhile to climb above the hut. Chamois are most frequently seen at dusk or in early morning, many hours before the crowds of hikers scare them away. The chamois are not overly nervous except during hunting season. Sometimes they will completely ignore a person who is sitting quietly by the side of the trail and will come within easy camera range. On the other hand, marmots, who burrow their homes into the hillside next to trails under rocks, often give a warning whistle when strangers approach.

There are several other worthwhile hikes in the Roseg Valley. For example, at the junction near the Hotel Roseg, a trail goes for 5 km to the Coaz Hütte, 2610 meters, where there are dramatic views of Roseg Glacier. For one of the greatest views in the Bernina Mountains, you can climb 4 km to Surlej Pass, 2755 meters, and then go 8 km downhill to St. Moritz, from where you can catch a bus back to Pontresina.

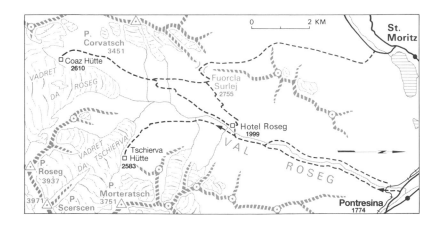

51 PIZ LANGUARD

Round trip 8 km, 5 miles
Hiking time 5 hours
High point 3262 meters, 10,699 feet

Elevation gain 1000 meters,
3280 feet
Map: Berninapass 269 or
Oberengadin, 1:60,000

The ibex, or steinbok as it is sometimes called, was almost extinct a few years ago, but with restrictions on hunting stringently enforced, they are now flourishing in certain areas of the Alps. Piz Languard is one of them, so load up the cameras.

By taking the chairlift from Pontresina you gain altitude quickly, but you sacrifice some of the fun of the long climb that begins up the valley. Although we did not hike the longer trail, we understand from good sources that it is well worth the effort. So consider traveling from Pontresina north to Punt Muragl, from where you can hike up or catch the *funicular* to Muottas Muragl, from where you pick up the Ibex Path, direction Piz Languard. Add about 3 hours to the 5-hour hike, particularly if you stop at the Chamanna Segantini restaurant.

From the terminal station of the Languard chairlift, elevation 2280 meters, follow the "PIZ LANGUARD" signs. The trail climbs steadily and, approximately halfway to the top, it crosses a stream. A little farther on it enters a nature preserve and switchbacks up the steep hillsides. At about 2900 meters, the Piz Languard trail meets another trail that goes to the Val da Fain. Keep left, and be especially careful in early summer crossing the frequent snow patches. Finally, the trail reaches the Berghaus Piz Languard, a 3200-meter-high hut and restaurant. Continue past the hut to the summit, which is 62 meters higher up. From that vantage point there are fine views of the Bernina and Vallais ranges. Depending on the time of year, you may or may not see the ibex.

It is more interesting to descend into the valley by a different route. One good possibility is to go via the Val da Fain, which will leave you on

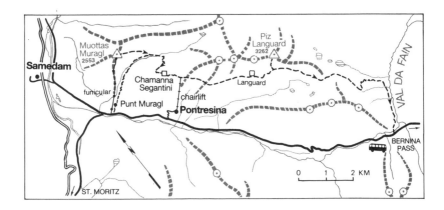

Ibex on the side of Piz Languard

the highway south of Pontresina. You can walk back to town on the trails paralleling the road, or hail a bus.

Hoping to photograph the ibex, we took this hike early in the summer, keeping our cameras ready at every turn of the trail. We did see a lone chamois, but that wasn't what we were looking for. At the Berghaus Piz Languard we were told that in June and July the big male ibex live in the rocky outcroppings lower on the mountain; they only move to higher ground in August and September. So, after soaking up the views, we hiked down. Sure enough, a short distance above the chairlift we found four male ibex grazing. Since they are not hunted, they are unafraid of humans, and we were able to approach them.

52   MORTERATSCH GLACIER

Round trip 8 km, 5 miles
Hiking time 4 hours
High point 2495 meters, 8184 feet
Elevation gain 600 meters,
1986 feet

Maps: Julierpass 268;
Berninapass 269;
Oberengadin, 1:60,000

This hike skirts by a glacier to a mountain hut with marvelous views of glaciers and peaks. In season, the trail is banked with lovely alpine rose. The classic photograph of flowers-in-foreground, glaciers-in-background has probably illustrated as many travel brochures and calendars as the Matterhorn. One short, well-traveled trail goes right up to the glacier snout itself and gives the hiker a clear picture of how glaciers in the Alps are receding. The main trail, however, skirts the snout and climbs to the hut.

From Pontresina, the trailhead can be reached by a short railroad ride or auto trip to Morteratsch. In either case, you go 5 km south toward the Bernina Pass, to the Morteratsch railroad station. Directly in front of the station is a trail sign on a gated service road, elevation 1896 meters. Hike on this road for a few hundred meters. The glacier snout trail heads left and is worth the short detour. After that, return and take the other trail, which switchbacks up a forested hillside and gains 200 vertical meters in 1 km. The trail levels a bit, then leaves the forest to traverse a steep hillside. This is the place to get out your camera, because 500 meters farther on views are blocked by a high lateral moraine. At about 3 km, the trail leaves the moraine and again steepens as it climbs a knoll. At 4 km, it reaches the Swiss Alpine Club's Boval hut at 2495 meters.

The outlooking meadow is an ideal place to relax and enjoy the scenery or to have lunch, which the hutkeeper will gladly serve you. Directly across from the hut, the Pers Glacier flows into the Morteratsch Glacier

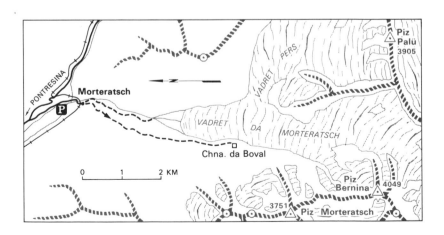

Morteratsch Glacier

and a whole circle of glacier-covered peaks, some more than 13,000 feet high, unfolds: Piz Bernina, Piz Bellavista, Piz Palü, and Piz Cambrena. Piz Boval is directly behind the hut. Only a few other Alpine areas offer such stunning views as these.

53 SCHÖNBERG

Loop trip 14 km, 8½ miles
Hiking time 5 hours
High point 2104 meters, 6901 feet

Elevation gain 704 meters,
2310 feet
Map: Liechtenstein Wanderkarte

The green and somewhat rounded summits of the Liechtenstein Alps offer front-row seating for panoramic views of the snow- and ice-covered Swiss Alps to the west and the towering rock crests of the Austrian Alps to the east. For the best views of the Austrian Alps, head up the Augstenberg (Hike No. 54). However, if you prefer the grandeur of the Swiss Alps, the ascent to the top of the Schönberg is a must.

From Vaduz, drive or take the bus 11.2 km up the steep mountain road to Steg. The trail begins above town, on the left-hand side of the road, in a narrow gorge. Parking is located on the right-hand side of the road, 200 meters beyond the trailhead, elevation 1400 meters. If riding the bus, show the driver where you want to go on the map and he will let you off at the correct spot.

The trail begins with a steep climb up the forested hillside. After 100 meters, cross a farm road and continue straight. Views begin with the first meadow, reached after 1½ km of climbing. Shortly beyond is the Bergle (1718 meters), a small farm where the trail disappears in the open meadows. Stay left of the farm building and contour across the meadow to a grass-covered saddle. Continue to contour the open hillside to the trail, which reappears about 100 meters beyond the saddle. Check for paint markings—if you do not find them you may be on a cow path; if so, head back to the saddle and try again.

The trail climbs and contours on the left side of a steep rib to reach the ridge crest and a trail intersection at 4½ km. The 2104-meter summit of the Schönberg is to your left, marked by a large cross. The final push to the rounded crest is an easy scramble across the meadow. There is no defined trail, so pick your own path.

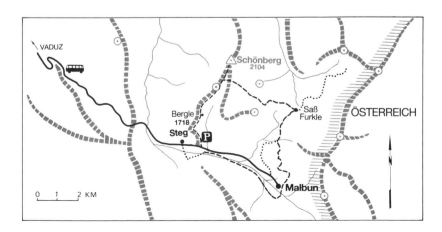

You now face a difficult choice. You may either check out all the views you missed on the way up by going back the way you came, or you may turn this hike into a loop and explore new vistas on the way down. For the loop trip, descend back to the saddle and then follow the well-defined trail that contours across a line of rugged cliffs. Exposed areas are secured with cables. At Saß Furkle, reached at 7 km, intersect a gravel road, 1785 meters. Go right and descend the road toward Malbun for 500 meters. At the first house, take the trail on the left and follow the scenic route down to Malbun.

At Malbun, the truly hardy may complete the loop by heading into town from the parking lot. In 200 meters, turn right on the Panorama Weg, which gains nearly 100 meters of elevation before heading down the valley on a gravel road. Follow the signs and descend along the Malbuner Bach toward Steg. Cross the river on a narrow bridge to meet the main road, and then head back uphill 200 meters to return to your starting point or head on down the road to catch the bus in Steg. You may also pick up the bus at Malbun if you prefer.

Trail intersection near the summit of the Schönberg

54 AUGSTENBERG

Round trip 10 km, 6 miles
Hiking time 5 hours
High point 2359 meters, 7738 feet
Elevation gain 800 meters,
2624 feet
Map: Liechtenstein Wanderkarte

International language

Considering that Liechtenstein consists of only 62 square miles, the principality has an impressive number of good hikes. Even more amazing is that, in a country smaller than the District of Columbia, solitude on the trails is not unusual. That, however, is not the case with this popular and scenic hike up the Augstenberg. A chairlift insures a constant stream of walkers along the ridge crest to the summit. Nevertheless, many people disdain the mechanical ascent and exercise their option of climbing all the way, both up and down.

From the capital city of Vaduz, where 3000 friendly people make up the entire population, drive or ride the post bus up the road signed "STEG UND MALBUN" for 13.6 km to its end. Park in the large lot at the entrance to Malbun, elevation 1602 meters.

From the upper end of the parking lot, head steeply uphill on a paved road, pass a stone church, and then traverse around the hillside and cross under the chairlift. The road turns to dirt and switchbacks up the hill to the top of the chairlift.

Near 2000 meters, with the summit in sight, head right on a trail signed "PFALZER-HÜTTE." This trail climbs to the ridge, where you will be joined by all those people who rode the chairlift up. Walk south and

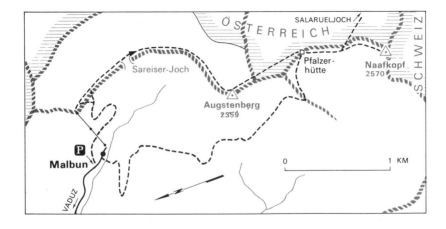

The town of Malbun from Augstenberg

then west along the rolling ridge crest, which has far more ups than downs. At 3½ km, after curving around the bowl-shaped valley above Malbun, reach the 2359-meter Augstenberg. From a 100-meter-high bluff are fine views of the Gamperdona Valley in Austria, the tiny farm village of Nenzinger-Himmel, and some Swiss summits in the Graubunden (Grissons) canton.

At this point you can retrace your steps and return to the valley, or continue southward along the ridge trail, contouring into Austria to the Pfalzer Hütte at Bettlerjoch, 2108 meters. Five major trails meet at the hut, making it an ideal base for further exploration. The most popular is the trail leading south to the 2570-meter summit of Naafkopf, where you can stand in three countries at the same time: Austria, Switzerland, and Liechtenstein. Another option is to follow the ridge trail eastward into Austria for outstanding views from Salarueljoch.

If your schedule doesn't allow for an overnight at the hut, from the five-trail junction, take the trail that heads west, toward Gritsch. This trail is just below the ridge you arrived on. After rounding the first major corner, the trail descends gradually to another junction. Stay right, climb over a shoulder of the Augstenberg, and then descend between the Hubel and the Nospitz. At 9½ km, join a service road that descends back to your starting point in Malbun.

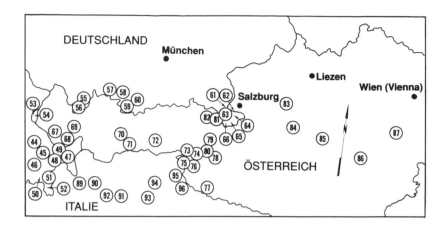

GERMANY

T he Alps make up only a very small part of Germany. They are a simple ruffle on the southwest portion of its border with Austria and are predominately limestone with gleaming gray or white summits and no glaciers. These strikingly beautiful mountains, known as the Bavarian Alps, are the home of several famous resort towns: Berchtesgaden, Garmisch-Partenkirchen, Füssen, and Oberstdorf.

Germans are enthusiastic walkers and the trails and gated mountain roads are always crowded. The trails are well signed and maintained. The system of *kletterwegs* (rock scramblers' trails—see the introduction to Austria for details) is not well developed. However, when the map indicates a dotted trail, you should be ready for some rock climbing along the steeper sections of the hike.

A few words of German are helpful when reading the maps and signs. A *tal* is a valley, a *bach* is a river, a *weg* or a *steg* is a trail, a *bahn* is a railroad or mountain lift, and a *hütte* is where you may buy a *wienerschnitzel*, apple strudel, or a *bier* and rent a room for the night.

Little evidence remains of the traditional mountain life in the Bavarian Alps. Tourism and the forest industry have taken over mountains; the high meadows bristle with ski lifts, while the lower hills are cut with roads used by the loggers. However, the enthusiam remains and the Germans proudly roam their mountains dressed in the traditional knickers and checked shirts.

In Bavaria it is best to exchange your money at a post office, which may be closed for up to 2 hours at noon. In fact, most of Bavaria still abides by the custom of closing stores and shops for a long lunch break.

Hirscheck (peak) from the summit of the Sonntagshorn (Hike No. 61)

Campgrounds are very crowded, especially in August. It is best to check in early and then go for your hike, rather than trying to find a place to stay in the evening. Private *Zimmers,* the German and Austrian equivalent to the bed and breakfast, offer moderate-priced accommodations in homes. Signs for *Zimmers* may be seen along the streets and highways. Tourist Information, found in all the larger towns, can help you with the more expensive lodging.

55   RUBIHORN

Loop trip 16 km, 10 miles	**Elevation gain 1107 meters,**
Hiking time 6 hours	**3632 feet**
High point 1957 meters, 6420 feet	**Map: Kompaß Wanderkarte 3**

All the elements that make hiking in the Alps so much fun and so addictive—cafés, the constant ringing of cow bells, small mountain farms tucked away in improbable places, open meadows, lakes, and excellent views from high, airy summits—are found on this hike to the summit of the Rubihorn. As with many hikes in the Alps, you have the option of hiking the whole way or gaining much of the elevation on a lift. And, like so many hikes in the Alps, several sections of this loop trail deteriorate into a scramble over exposed rocks, a challenge for the surefooted hiker but very difficult for anyone who does not have a good head for heights.

In Oberstdorf, follow the signs to the Nebelhornbahn, a popular ski lift. From the lift station, take the first turn left, cross a bridge, and follow the narrow road uphill. At the base of the ski jump, the road divides; go left to a large parking lot, elevation 850 meters.

The hike begins on a paved road. After 150 meters go left on a trail signed "CAFÉ BREITENBERG." The trail to the café branches off to the right at 700 meters. Stay left, climb above the café, and then traverse through forest across the lower slopes of the Rubihorn. At 5½ km is a major junction with the trail from Rubi (which is actually a dirt road) and, shortly after, with the trail from Reichenbach. Follow the road upvalley to the 1149-meter Gaisalpe, a popular restaurant located 6 km from the start.

The road ends and the trail continues on, climbing steeply above Gaisalpe through open meadows. The tread of the trail is rough, switchbacking and scrambling over slippery rocks, until, at 7½ km, it arrives at Unter Gaisalpsee, a pretty lake at 1550 meters. Anyone who rode the lift up joins the hike here.

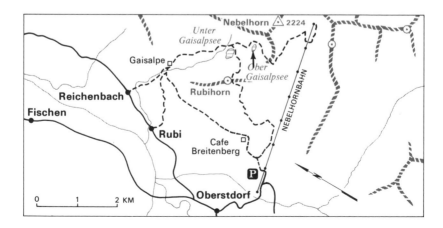

The summit of the Rubihorn

After a rest at the lake it is time for a decision. If you thought the trail to the lake was difficult or unpleasant, forget about the Rubihorn and head on to the very scenic Ober Gaisalpsee. However, if you are still waiting to be challenged, follow the trail down to the lake, pass the tempting benches, and head up the very steep trail to the Rubihorn. Near the top, at around 10 km, the trail crosses a narrow, rocky saddle. Head right for the final push to the top and enjoy the magnificent view.

When you are ready to head down, retrace your steps to the saddle and then continue straight up the rocks and along the ridge crest to a second saddle. A short side trip from the saddle, on a trail secured with cables and a ladder, leads to the 1953-meter summit of Gaisalphorn. The loop trail heads down, with a rough start over a rock outcrop, and then settles into well-graded switchbacks.

At 14 km, with the cable-car station in view, turn right, off the main trail and descend a narrow path to the service road. Follow this road and the hordes of fellow walkers back to the ski jump.

Baad and Derrenjoch (river valley)

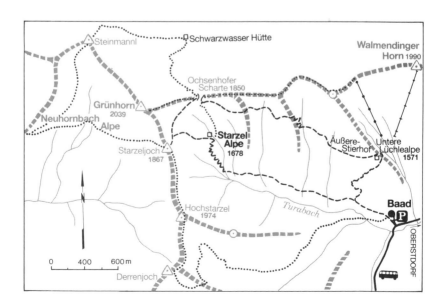

56 OCHSENHOFER SCHARTE LOOP

Basic loop trip 10 km, 6½ miles
Hiking time 4 hours
High point 1867 meters, 6125 feet

Elevation gain 623 meters,
2044 feet
Map: Kompaß Wanderkarte 3

The loop described here is just a sampler of what can be done in this enticing valley that simply seems to invite off-trail exploration, tempting hikers to wander along ridgetops and then push on to the summits. Suggestions for longer hikes are given below.

The trailhead is located at the southern end of the Kleinwalsertal, a narrow valley with a curious history. Until 1930, when the first road was built, the valley was isolated from the rest of Europe, leaving the people to develop a style of dress and housing uniquely their own. Today the valley is part of Austria but can only be reached, by road, from Germany. Perhaps for this reason the currency used in the valley is the Deutschmark, even for buying Austrian postage stamps.

To reach the Kleinwalsertal, drive through Oberstdorf on Route 19. Continue to follow Route 19 as it climbs into this small Austrian valley. Pass the Austrian and German customs house, generally unoccupied, and continue upvalley to road's end at Baad. If arriving by public transportation, ride the train to Oberstdorf and then catch a bus.

From the parking lot at Baad, elevation 1244 meters, walk up the main road through town. The road divides just below the church. Go left on Starzelweg. At the outskirts of town, find a well-marked trail on the right and head uphill. This is a popular descent route from the Walmendinger Horn Bahn (a cable car originating in Mittelberg), so expect a lot of company on the trail, all heading in the other direction.

The trail climbs steadily for 1 km to Untere Lüchlealpe, 1571 meters. Go left here, heading to Außere-Stierhof. At 2½ km from Baad, go left again for a ½-km traverse across an open meadow to yet another junction. Go right.

Ochsenhofer Scharte, a small 1850-meter pass with a view north into the Schwarzwassertal, is reached at 4 km and, with it, several choices. The basic loop route follows the trail across the meadows to Starzeljoch, a 1867-meter pass located 700 meters to the southwest. However, if you wish to vastly extend the hike, check out the loop route that descends to Schwarzwasser Hütte, climbs over Steinmannl, descends to Neuhornbach Alpe, and then climbs back to Starzeljoch, adding 7 km to the basic hike. For experienced hikers, wandering over the ridgetops is another option from Ochsenhofer Scharte. Instead of following the trail, scramble over the 2039-meter Grünhorn to Starzeljoch.

Once at Starzeljoch, hikers are faced with another temptation to explore, this time on a rough route over Hochstarzel to Derrenjoch, where a good trail heads down the valley to Baad.

From Starzeljoch, the basic loop descends to Starzel Alp, down a steep trail into the valley, and along the Turabach back to Baad.

57   TEGELBERG

Loop trip 15 km, 9½ miles
Hiking time 7 hours
High point 1707 meters, 5599 feet

Elevation gain 900 meters,
2953 feet
Map: Kompaß Wanderkarte 4

Of all the famous sights of Germany, none is as well known as Neuschwanstein, a fairy-tale castle built in the Bavarian Alps in the middle 1800s by King Ludwig II. Although most people visit this area to see the castle, the hills behind the castle offer excellent hiking. Shunning the nearby cable lift up the Tegelberg, the nearest mountain to the castle, hundreds of tourists and hikers climb up and down the trails to see, visit, and search for the best photographic views of Neuschwanstein Castle and the neighboring Hohenschwangau Castle. Along the way, intrepid photographers and hikers pass by a gorge, waterfalls, forests, chamois, and fascinating limestone formations and—when they reach the summit—find an aerial view of lakes, farms, and villages.

From the town of Füssen, follow the signs to Hohenschwangau and the castles. If traveling by car, either park in one of the pay lots at the base of the royal castles or along the side roads a kilometer or so away (elevation 850 meters). The yellow castle is Hohenschwangau. Pass this one and follow the stream of tourists up either the steep road or the trail to Neuschwanstein, the white castle on the hill. At the base of the castle, keep to the right and climb to the bus stop for the tour buses. Go left to the Marienbrücke. At 1 km cross the high foot bridge and start up the trail, leaving the majority of the tourists behind.

The trail is narrow as it heads into a seemingly endless series of switchbacks. At first the castle can be seen through the trees, but then the trail turns a corner and views are to the south. The hillside gets steeper. The trail climbs between pillars of limestone where the handrail is a welcome aid. At 5 km the trail forks. Both trails head for the 1707-

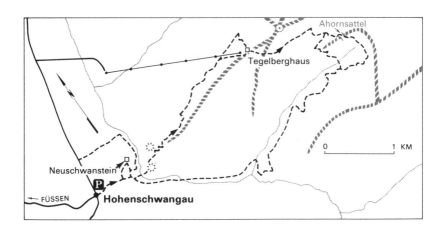

Neuschwanstein Castle

meter summit of the Tegelberg; the right-hand trail is shorter and a bit steeper.

The views from the summit platform are spectacular. Farms, lakes, and cities are to be seen more than 1000 vertical meters below. From the summit, take the trail heading southeast toward the Ahornsattel. In 1 km you reach a trail junction. The shortest way back is to the right; however, for the best views, detour left over Ahornsattel with a side trip to Ahornspitze. Stay right at the next intersection and rejoin the main trail in 1½ km. The meadows are verdant here, the forests thick, and herds of chamois live in the rocks and meadows. At 10 km the trail widens into a gravel road, which follows the Deutenhauserbach to intersect the well-used road paralleling the Pollat River. Near 13 km the river plunges dramatically through a steep gorge from which one has an astonishing view of Neuschwanstein Castle. The road climbs a bit to reach the tourist bus stop station; go right here and join the hordes heading down toward the castle.

If time and energy allow, return via a side trail. Descend to about 200 meters above the castle and then go right on a well-maintained but unmarked path that drops into the gorge. Follow this path downstream on a catwalk bolted to the cliffs. At the base of the gorge, turn left to return to the parking area.

The summit of the Klammspitz

58   KLAMMSPITZ

Round trip 20 km, 12½ miles
Hiking time 5 hours
High point 1924 meters, 6312 feet

Elevation gain 964 meters,
3163 feet
Map: Kompaß Wanderkarte 5

On a good weekend hundreds of hikers, including small children attached to their parents by short ropes, climb to the 1924-meter summit of Klammspitz. It's a Bavarian specialty, like the passion plays at the city of Oberammergau, about 15 kilometers away, which occur once every ten years; the next performance will be in the year 2000.

Even though it is popular, this is not an easy trip. The hike is fairly long and strenuous, and, on the final pitches, the trail peters out. The summit push more nearly resembles a rock scramble than a Sunday outing with grandparents. On wet days the climb to the limestone summit is slippery and should be avoided.

From Highway 23 between Oberammergau and Garmisch-Partenkirchen, turn west toward Reutte and travel to the Linderhof Schloß. On the west side of the castle parking lot (fee charged) is a small stream. Cross the bridge to the overflow parking lot and go right, following the stream to the trailhead, elevation 960 meters.

The trail, which is a steep jeep road, reaches a well-developed forest road at 1 km. Head across the forest road and then on up the jeep road, which switchbacks through the forest. At 4½ km is an open meadow and the first of many imposing views. At 1602 meters, ½ km farther, reach the Brunnenkopf-Häuser café, where the jeep road ends. The trail traverses west around the open hillside above the café, then descends 100 meters to a green meadow before starting the final push to the summit, which involves weaving around a buttress and then climbing the rocky back side.

In addition to fine panoramic views, watch for chamois, which love to show off their climbing skills to appreciative audiences of tired hikers.

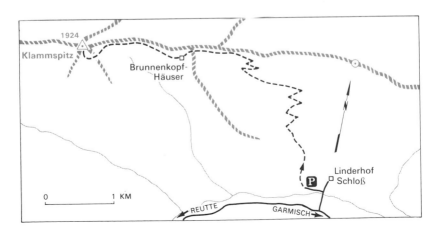

59   REINTALANGER HÜTTE

Round trip 28 km, 17½ miles
Hiking time 8 hours
High point 1367 meters, 4484 feet

Elevation gain 567 meters,
**   1860 feet**
Map: Kompaß Wanderkarte 5

This is a long, pleasant hike up a beautiful valley walled in by peaks whose sheer rock faces rise straight from the valley floor. Paralleling a rushing stream most of the way, the trail passes through a narrow canyon, by a lake and a waterfall, and through a thick forest before reaching open meadows. Views are splendid along the entire trail.

From Garmisch-Partenkirchen, drive or take the city bus to the *skistadion* (ski stadium) on the east side of Partenkirchen. Navigation through town is accomplished by following the "MITTENWALD" signs. If arriving by train, get off at the Kainzenbad station and walk to the *skistadion,* elevation 800 meters.

From the *skistadion* walk along a paved road. In tourist season, you'll have no trouble finding the way: just follow the crowds and the horse-drawn taxis. At Wildenau (1½ km), the paved road ends. Cross a bridge, turn right, and follow the paved trail marked "PARTNACHKLAMM," which parallels the river a short distance and then divides. The lower route, a toll trail, has been hacked out of the sheer canyon walls. It passes through dark tunnels just above the river, which twists and rolls below. The canyon is damp from the spray of waterfalls that come off both sides. If you prefer to avoid the toll, take the upper trail and climb steeply, with good views into the canyon.

At 3 km, the trail joins a dirt road heading toward Reintalanger Hütte, paralleling the Partnach River, with frequent views of the mountains ahead. The road ends at 7½ km and the real trail begins. The valley is narrower now, boxed in by cliffs. At 9 km the trail to Schachenhaus branches off to the left. Shortly beyond is Bock Hütte. The trail num-

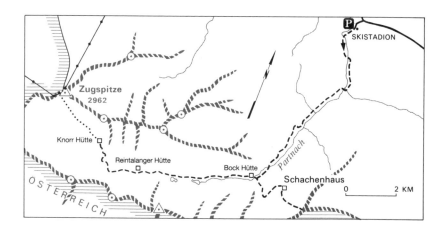

Partnach River near Bock Hütte

ber changes here from R1 to R2 or 801, the forest thins, and the view expands.

At 11½ km the river is blocked by talus, forming several shallow lakes. After passing the first lake at 13 km, the trail climbs over a waterfall to meadows and at 14 km reaches Reintalanger Hütte, 1367 meters.

If time, energy, and weather permit, continue on to the 2051-meter Knorr Hütte, located in the lower section of a rocky basin and surrounded by tall peaks, including the Zugspitze, at 2962 meters Germany's highest mountain.

60   KROTTENKOPF

Round trip 24 km, 15 miles
Hiking time 9 hours
High point 2086 meters, 6844 feet

Elevation gain 1236 meters,
  4055 feet
Map: Kompaß Wanderkarte 5

Not very far from the crowds of the Garmisch-Partenkirchen area is a quiet area with lovely forests, large meadows, and magnificent views. Tourists rarely visit here because, although the scenery is good, it does

Meadow below Kuhalm

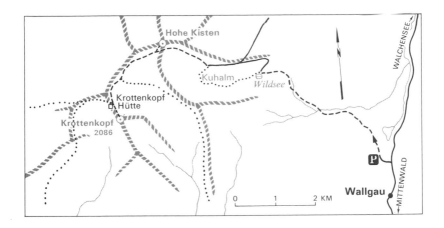

not compete with the ravishing views at the top of the cable car in Garmisch-Partenkirchen. However, as the local people have long known, the hiking is much better.

Unfortunately, logging roads have stolen some of the pristine feeling from the area. But since only loggers and farmers are allowed on these roads, the intrusion has remained at acceptable levels.

Drive or take the bus from Garmisch-Partenkirchen and head east 20 km toward Mittenwald. At a major junction 9 km south of Mittenwald, turn north on Highway 11 for 2 km to the small town of Wallgau. Just 200 meters north of town, find a forest road on the left (west) signed "KROTTENKOPF" and "SIMETSBERG." Turn here and park along the road where convenient, elevation 850 meters.

While some areas are notable for their deer and others for chamois, birds, or views, this area must be noted for its ants. Several dozen huge anthills line the trail, so start out with a steady pace and plan not to stop until you reach the high meadows.

Walk up the main road, passing a gate and then heading through the forest. At 1 km is a junction; take the uphill fork. After 3 km, cross a stream, then leave the road and follow a rough trail that climbs steeply along the right side of the stream. In the next kilometer the trail gains more than 300 meters of elevation and crosses another major road. The climb slackens a bit at 4½ km where the trail reaches another well-used road. Go left here and walk around the tiny Wildsee, 1392 meters.

Beyond the lake, the trail follows the valley up a ravine to the crest of a low ridge and then into open meadows at the base of Kuhalm, 1650 meters. Cross the meadow and pick up a service road, which passes several farmhouses. Beyond the buildings, the trail traverses across the open slopes of Hohe Kisten, a high point on the ridge with a large cross on top.

The trail continues with an easy traverse for the final 2½ km to Krottenkopf Hütte, 1955 meters. From the hut it is a quick ½-km jaunt to the 2086-meter summit of Krottenkopf, where you may enjoy excellent views in quiet solitude. If you have a good map and some extra time, consider making a loop on your return to Wallgau.

Sign near the summit of the Sonntagshorn

61   SONNTAGSHORN

Round trip 16 km, 10 miles
Hiking time 9 hours
High point 1961 meters, 6432 feet

Elevation gain 1403 meters,
   4601 feet
Map: Kompaß Wanderkarte 12

Don't let the name of the mountain fool you—Sunday's Horn is a popular destination every day of the week. Most people approach the mountain from Austria, where the summit is a short hike from the Ennsmann-Kaser café near the resort town of Lofer. Only slightly less popular and considerably longer are the approaches from the small town of Laubau, in Germany. Both approaches from Laubau involve a rock scramble near the top. The approach suggested here is the most interesting and begins on the Austrian–German border. The route climbs through a forested valley on a trail that is rarely used, by European standards, and then heads up over open meadows with outstanding vistas over Germany and Austria.

From Berchtesgaden, drive Highway 305 for 14 km to its intersection with Highway 21. Go left for 8 km to Steinpaß on the German–Austrian border. Near the border-crossing station, stay in the right lane. Just before the guard station, turn right on a narrow road and head uphill for 200 meters. At the edge of a bridge over the Steinbach, find a forest road on the left. Park here, elevation 558 meters.

The route begins by following the gravel logging road along the valley floor. At this point you are actually in Austria but will return to Germany when the road crosses the river. After 1½ km the road divides. Stay left and cross a bridge back into Austria. The road ends and the trail begins by heading steeply up the forested hillside. Red and white stripes mark the narrow trail, which switchbacks and traverses.

Views begin after the trail crosses the Roßkar Bach at 4 km and climbs through a logging clearing. In another ½ km the trail enters open meadows and disappears under the grass and alpine flowers. Continue to climb straight up the hillside until you reach a farm road and then go left to the ridge crest.

For those who have done enough climbing for the day, the 1650-meter ridgetop, at 6 km, is a fine turn-around point. Views from here are nearly as good as those from the summit, with the farmlands, rolling hills, and rugged peaks of Austria spread out below your feet.

The determined peak baggers should follow Trail 21 to the right, along the crest of the ridge. At 6½ km, meet the major trail from the Ennsmann-Kaser café and head up the excellently graded path for the final 1½ km to the summit of the 1961-meter Sonntagshorn. The views expand here to include Germany as well as Austria. Note the Reiter Alpe to the southeast and Loferer and Leoganger Stenberge to the south.

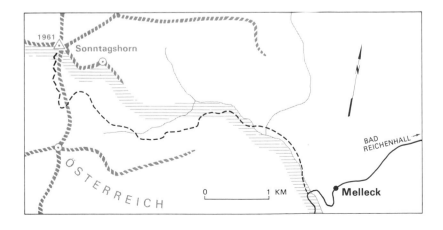

62   REITER ALPE

Round trip 14 km, 9 miles
Hiking time 6½ hours
High point 1557 meters, 5107 feet

Elevation gain 607 meters,
1991 feet
Map: Kompaß Wanderkarte 14

The Reiter Alpe, split by the unseen line of the German–Austrian border, is an ideal place to spend a day or a week. On the topographic map the alpe appears to be a level plateau at the crest of cliffs that tower 1000 meters above the surrounding farmland. In reality, the plateau is characterized by depressions, with steep sides and high peaks. Terrain is extremely rugged, made so by the predominance of weathered limestone. Meadows are spotted with white and pink outcroppings, many of which are textured with long, narrow grooves created by water. Days may be spent wandering to the ridgetops for views and exploring the odd rock formations of the alpe.

The suggested hike goes as far as the Neue Traunsteiner Hütte, an excellent overnight base for explorations to the ridge crest where the views are truly splendid and the possibilities for wandering nearly endless. The strong hiker, with a good head for heights, may turn the basic hike into an excellent 20-km loop.

To reach the Reiter Alpe trailhead, drive or take the bus northwest on Highway 305 from Berchtesgaden. At the summit of Schwarzbachwacht, a 950-meter pass, turn left, off the highway, and park in the large gravel lot.

From the right side of the parking area, find a narrow road behind the buildings. The road heads downhill for a short distance and then forks. Take the road on the left, signed "NEUE TRAUNSTEINER HÜTTE," also

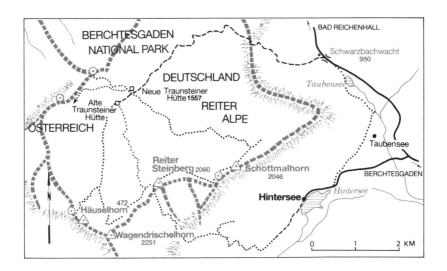

Sheep on Reiter Steinberg

called the "KARL-MERKENSCHLAGER-HAUS." At the next fork go right and after 1 km enter the Nationalpark Berchtesgaden. The road ends here and the trail begins, climbing with a series of switchbacks, stairs, and ladders. After 4 km and a long series of false summits is a small glen with several old ruined buildings. The trail levels off a bit, enters Reiter Alpe, and begins working its way through and around limestone sinkholes. At 7 km is Neue Traunsteiner Hütte, 1557 meters.

Now it is time to explore. Just across the meadow, in Austria, is the Alte Traunsteiner Hütte, which is no longer open on a daily basis. The best course is to head up to the ridge crests and enjoy the views. Experienced hikers who wish to complete the loop should walk across the meadow to Austria and follow Trail 472, the Steinberggaße, up Reiter Steinberg. At the summit, follow the Böselsteig, which weaves its way down the cliffs with the help of a few cables and ladders to the floor of the Klausbach Valley. The trail ends at a paved road on the valley floor. Go left, out of the national park, and down the valley to an intersection. Stay left here, walk around Hintersee, climb the gentle rise, and follow signs to Taubersee. From Taubersee it's only another ½ km to Schwarzbachwacht and the end of the loop.

63   BLAUEIS HÜTTE

Round trip 10 km, 6 miles
Hiking time 4 hours
High point 1750 meters, 5740 feet

Elevation gain 1000 meters,
  3280 feet
Map: Kompaß Wanderkarte 14

Elements such as beautiful scenery, a short and excellent trail, and two huts where refreshments may be purchased combine to make Blaueis Hütte one of the most popular hikes in the Berchtesgaden area. The hut lies at the edge of a hanging valley, carved by a massive glacier. Unlike the surrounding areas with their hills of broken and weathered limestone, the rock walls here are sheer and massive, towering above the valley and dwarfing the hut and its inhabitants.

Drive or take the bus on Highway 305, northwest from Berchtesgaden to the town of Ramsau. On the outskirts of town, 500 meters west of the post office, turn left and cross a stream on a one-lane bridge to reach a parking lot and the trailhead, elevation 750 meters. (A second trailhead is located another 4 km upvalley, near Hintersee. Both trails are good and eventually join.)

The trail begins as a wide, moderately steep forest road. After walking 800 meters, take a right fork on a steep wagon road, passing a number of signed intersections. Stay with the road until it ends, and then head uphill on a well-graded trail. At 2½ km the trail joins the jeep road from Hintersee. At 3 km, pass a small restaurant at Schärten-alm, 1362 meters.

The trail passes above the restaurant and contours around the hill, where it is suspended from the side of a cliff on a wooden bridge. At 4 km the service road ends and a trail switchbacks up the final hill to Blaueis Hütte at 5 km, elevation 1750 meters. This is a base camp for climbers and a good place to watch them in action.

All the trails continuing on from the hut are *kletterwegs,* difficult

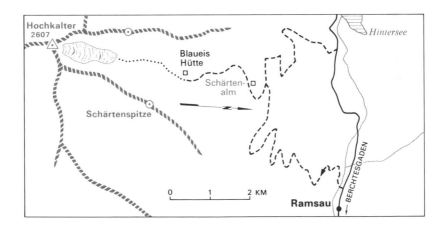

Alpine chalet near Blaueis Hütte

routes designed for surefooted hikers and climbers who have a good head for heights. However, one trail can be followed without difficulty for 1 km above the hut to the edge of the glacier, last remnant of the mighty ice flow that carved the valley.

64   WIMBACHGRIES HÜTTE

One way to Königssee 19 km,
12 miles
Hiking time 1 to 2 days
High point 1774 meters, 5820 feet

Elevation gain 1014 meters,
3327 feet
Map: Kompaß Wanderkarte 14

This is a popular 16-km, one-day hike to Wimbachgries Hütte or an equally popular 19-km, two-day hike over a 1774-meter pass to the shores of the fjordlike Königssee. No matter which option you chose, the scenery and trails are excellent.

If hiking the one-day option, drive or take the bus from Berchtesgaden west on Highway 305 to the little village of Schwaben. At the Wimbachbruckle bus stop, turn left (south) on a narrow road, of same name, and cross the Ramsauer Ache on a single-lane car bridge to the parking lot, elevation 760 meters. For the two-day option, leave your car at the Königssee parking lot in Berchtesgaden and take the bus to Schwaben.

Continue up the road on foot. When the road divides, stay right and chug up the steep grade—the steepest of the entire hike. The pavement

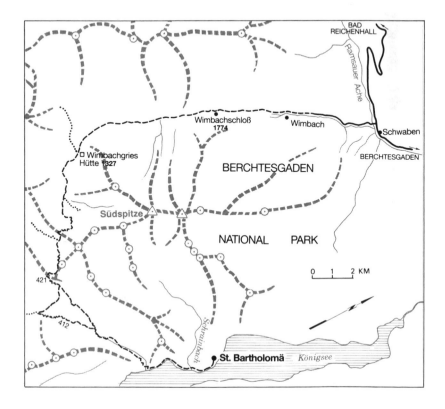

Curious deer inspecting guest at Wimbachgries Hütte

ends when the road leaves the village, and a gravel service road continues up the valley. At 500 meters is an intersection. To the right, the service road continues upvalley to the hut. On the left, a trail descends to the Wimbachklamm, a toll trail through a narrow gorge with a wood-planked walkway built out from the walls to give access to the waterfall. The toll trail rejoins the gravel road 300 meters up the valley.

At 2 km, the road passes a waterworks. Above this point the river disappears underground. At 4 km, you arrive at the Wimbachschloß, 937 meters, a former royal hunting lodge that is now a restaurant. The road continues its scenic course up the valley, paralleling and then moving to the center of the dry riverbed. Views continue to improve. As you climb farther into the valley, rocky spires come into view.

A small hikers' and climbers' shelter is passed at 6 km and at 8 km the road arrives at Wimbachgries Hütte, 1327 meters. This cozy little hut is located on an oasis of green amid barren peaks and the rock-covered riverbed. A wide lawn and the forested hillside behind the hut combine to give the area a parklike atmosphere. Fresh water is available from a pipe next to the hut. Most two-day hikers spend the night here.

To continue on, head upvalley on an excellent though poorly signed trail. It begins by crossing the valley and heading up on the west side of the riverbed. Near 9 km, the trail recrosses the riverbed and then begins its climb to the 1774-meter pass where the trail divides. Go straight,

Buck grazing in meadow

Wimbach valley

following Trail 421 as it descends through pocket-size meadows and winds its way over and around the weathered limestone. Ladders aid the descent.

At 12½ km is an intersection and a choice. The left-hand trail is the shortest, but requires skirting across a very exposed cliff with the help of a ladder and a cable. The right-hand trail contours south to intercept Trail 412 and then descends with a long series of switchbacks. The two trails rejoin at 14 km, elevation 980 meters, and continue down (occasionally very steeply) along the Schrain Bach to the Königssee. Follow the multitude of tourists along the shores of the lake to St. Bartholoma where you may catch the boat back to Königssee and the parking lot. Note: The last boat leaves at 7:00 P.M.

65 KÖNIGSSEE

One way 11 km, 7 miles	Elevation gain 800 meters,
Hiking time 5 hours	2624 feet
High point 1420 meters, 4658 feet	Map: Kompaß Wanderkarte 14

South of Berchtesgaden is a dazzling glacier-carved lake with the clearest water in Europe, rightly known as Königssee, or the King's Lake. With cliffs rising 800 meters straight up from the shore, this lake is as impressive as any fjord in Norway, New Zealand, or Alaska. For the tourist, the boat ride from the town of Königssee to the head of the lake is a prime attraction. For the hiker and explorer, the hills above the lake offer numerous outstanding trails.

The most scenic of these trails is the climb to Kührointalm. This trail looks impossible from the water, beginning at St. Bartholomä Church, a charming structure with two onion-top steeples and a restaurant, and climbing to the top of a sheer 800-meter cliff with superb views of the lake and the entire Watzmann Range. This difficult climb is accomplished with the aid of ladders, wooden bridges, cables, and sculptured handholds. If you or anyone in your party is not comfortable with heights, or if it is a wet day, take a different trail. As the climb to Kührointalm is exposed to the sunshine most of the day, early morning or late afternoon (with an overnight stay at the hut) are the best times to do the hike.

Drive or take the bus to Berchtesgaden and then follow the signs to Königssee and buy a one-way ticket to St. Bartholomä, where the hike starts at 604 meters.

In St. Bartholomä walk around the left side of the church and restaurant and follow the lakeshore until the trail divides. Continue straight on a trail signed "NUR FÜR GEÜBTE," meaning for "for the experienced only." For the next 4 km, follow this rough, rocky, steep trail up the cliffs

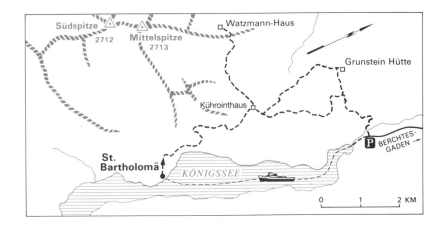

St. Bartholomä and the Königssee

for 600 vertical meters and then into the trees for another 200 nearly vertical meters. Cross open spaces on steeply tilted wooden trestles, clamber up ladders to narrow ledges, and, above all, enjoy the view of the lake, which is almost directly below your feet.

At the top of the climb the trail becomes a service road. The road climbs gently to the Kührointhaus, where you may buy a snack, rest shaky legs, and enjoy a view of 2713-meter-high Mittelspitze in the Watzmann Range. Above, visible on a shoulder of the mountain, is the Watzmann Haus.

From the Kührointhaus there are several routes back to the start. The most interesting is via the 1304-meter Grünstein with its view over Berchtesgaden. The quickest way back is Trail 443, signed "SCHÖNAU UND KÖNIGSSEE." This broad, sometimes steep, and muddy path ends in a maze of residential roads from which hikers must find their way back to the Königssee parking lot.

GERMANY
Berchtesgaden

66   HAGEN GEBIRGE

Round trip to Hoher Göll 21 km, 13 miles
Hiking time 9 hours
High point 2522 meters, 8274 feet

Elevation gain 1422 meters, 4665 feet
Map: Kompaß Wanderkarte 14

On a clear day this outstanding ridge walk along the crest of the Hagen
Gebirge offers some of the best views in the Berchtesgaden area. From
the summit of Hoher Göll, the 2522-meter-high point of the ridge, panoramic vistas extend deep into Germany and as far over Austria as the
ice-capped Dachstein Range.

The entire hike is an all-day proposition that can be shortened or altered to fit your time, energy, and skill. Two of many hiking options are
given below. Pick the one that suits you best.

The most scenic version, a one-way traverse, starts from the Roßfeld
Toll Road and follows a good trail 1½ km to Purtschellerhaus. The trail
ends here and a *kletterweg* (scramblers' trail) continues on to the summit
of Hoher Göll, climbing up steep rock faces, traversing cliffs, and relying
on cables and ladders that start too late and end too soon. This route is
only for the surefooted who are comfortable with heights and rock scram-

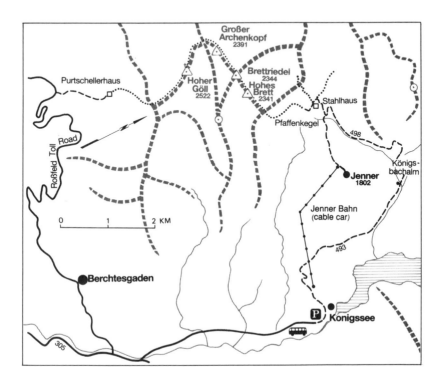

Kletterweg near the summit of Hoher Göll

bling. Do not attempt this hike unless the slippery limestone rock is absolutely dry. From Hoher Göll a rough trail is followed along the ridge crest to Stahlhaus, where a service road descends to Königssee.

If you feel you can handle this difficult route, leave your car in the parking lot at Königssee, just south of Berchtesgaden, and catch the bus up past Obersalzberg to the Ahornkaser bus stop on the Roßfeld road. Tourist Information can help with times and schedules.

The second and much easier option requires only a minor amount of rock scrambling, but does require a considerable amount of energy for climbing the rough and steep trail to the ridge crest. Drive or take the bus to the Königssee parking lot, elevation 604 meters. Buy a one-way ticket and ride the Jenner Bahn (a cable car) to its top at 1802 meters. Walk the open meadows across the ridge to Stahlhaus. Go past the café and then turn left and head up on a badly eroded trail. Climb pass Pfaffenkegel to reach 2341-meter Hohes Brett in 2 very steep km. If the trail seemed difficult to you up to now, make this summit your destination and enjoy the views over the German and Austrian alps. If you continue on, views change, but they never get better.

From Hohes Brett the rough trail follows the ridge east, passing 2344-meter Brettriedel and 2391-meter Großer Archenkopf. At 6 km from the top of the Jennerbahn is a steep descent with cables, then a short 5-meter scramble down a band of rocks. From here the way is easy. The trail traverses the head of a rock-strewn valley and then climbs past a minor summit marked with a cross to reach the true summit of Hoher Göll, also marked with a cross. To return, hike back down the ridge to Stahlhaus and then follow Trails 498 and 493 to the parking lot at Königssee.

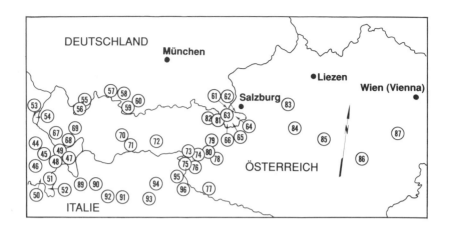

AUSTRIA

T he Alps of Austria are divided into three distinct chains that run east to west. The Northern Limestone Alps extend almost to Vienna and are separated from the High Alps in the center of the country by the Inn, Salzach, and Enns rivers. The High Alps are formed of crystalline rock. Many summits, including the 3797-meter Großglockner, Austria's highest, are glacier-covered. The third chain lies on the border with Italy and Slovenia and is called the Southern Limestone Alps.

The Austrians are enthusiastic hikers and the mountains are criss-crossed with well-maintained trails. The Austrians have a well-developed system of mountain huts (hotels). Hikers usually have a choice of room types: double, four-person, or dormitory style. Food is generally good; however, most huts have their own specialties. To find out about this, ask the hut manager or one of the Austrian guests.

Trails in Austria are well signed, usually with a destination and a suggested walking time. The *kletterwegs* (also called *klettersteigs*) are a popular type of trail where hiking is combined with easy rock climbing in the safest manner possible. These routes vary in difficulty but rarely in quality. Most *kletterwegs* have paint marks that lead you in a dot-to-dot fashion up or across exposed cliffs. When the going gets difficult, ladders, cables, or hand- and footholds are added. If you enjoy this type of hiking, carry a basic kit containing a harness, slings, and carabiners so you may clip into the cables if needed. Many of the difficult *kletterwegs* are signed at the start as "NUR FÜR GEÜBTE" (for the experienced only).

Mountain taxis are another feature of the Austrian Alps. These taxis are moderately priced and usually large enough to carry an entire hiking

Summit cross on Madelz-Kogel (Hike No. 80)

party from the trailhead to the town or the train station. If you wish to call a mountain taxi, stop in at a restaurant or guest house near the trailhead and ask if this service is available.

Plank bridge across the Valzifenzer Bach in Wintertal

67   WINTER TAL

Loop trip 16 km, 10 miles
Hiking time 6 hours
High point 2485 meters, 8151 feet

Elevation gain 1000 meters,
   3280 feet
Map: Kompaß Wanderkarte 41

Green meadows, fields of alpine rose, and tantalizing views make Winter
Tal the kind of valley that lures your feet off the trail—to wander over
the next green ridge or up a rounded summit or two. Winter Tal is beautiful in the summer when the huge meadows are reddened by fields of alpine rose and framed by large snowdrifts. If you wish to stay out a day or
two, there are plenty of camping opportunities as long as the water flows
(until mid-August) and the hike may be extended to Silvretta Stausee if
you are so inclined.

From the town of Bludenz, at the far western extremity of Austria, drive or take the post bus south on Highway 188 for 16 km and then turn right on Highway 192 for 10 km to the Schalbergbahn chairlift at the upper end of Gargellen. Continue uphill for 500 meters to a "Y" in the road. Get off the bus or park your car in the small lot at the intersection, elevation 1485 meters.

Head up the middle of the "Y" on a dirt service road that parallels the Valzinfenzer Bach. At 500 meters the road crosses the river. Leave the road and follow a trail up the right side of the river for 1 km to Madrisa Hütte and then cross and walk the now unavoidable service road on the left side of the valley.

At 4 km pass a waterworks where a trail climbs over Schlappinerjoch into Switzerland. Stay on the service road for another 500 meters and follow the road across the river. The road ends at last after recrossing the river at about 5 km. At 6 km, 2221 meters, reach a group of farmhouses set amidst alpine meadows with splendid views of the snowy slopes of the Rotbühlspitz. For the loop trip, continue upward. The trail soon becomes hard to distinguish in the wet meadows and boulder fields. To avoid getting lost, follow the paint marks and go dot-to-dot to Valzifenzerjoch, a 2485-meter pass.

From the pass, the trail descends 100 meters and then contours over a boulder-strewn ridge. Snow often lingers here until August; gaiters and an ice axe may be useful. At 11 km, the trail passes a small hut and then crosses a deep, bubbling creek to reach an intersection. The loop hike goes left and descends through Vergaldner Tal, first on trail, then on farm road. Trail 302, to the right at the intersection, heads east to Silvretta Stausee.

The loop trail reaches 1820-meter Vergaldner Alm at 14 km, where a spur trail takes off to Heimbühl Spitz. At 15½ km, with the town of Gargellen in sight, the trail divides. Stay left at the first intersection for 20 meters and then take a right. Descend to the Hotel Vergalden and then walk the paved road back to the start.

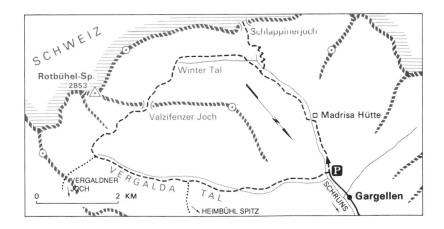

68 WIESBADENER HÜTTE

Loop trip 13 km, 8 miles
Hiking time 5 to 6 hours
High point 2701 meters, 8862 feet

Elevation gain 665 meters,
2185 feet
Map: Kompaß Wanderkarte 41

From the very start the views are magnificent, and it seems unlikely that they can improve. But they do. All in all, this is a great hike. It is short, has very little elevation gain, and best of all, can be turned into a loop hike.

From Bludenz, head southeast on Highway 188 for 42 km to Silvretta Stausee and park in the large lot at the edge of the reservoir, elevation 2036 meters. Note: The toll to drive the road is very high. The only way to avoid the charge is to arrive very late at night or extremely *early* in the morning.

From the parking lot, walk across the high concrete dam and then along the west shore of the lake. Several junctions are passed; stay left. At 3 km you meet the east-side trail; keep right. Ahead is Ochsentaler Glacier with its many crevasses and long snowfields. Near 4 km, a second broad glacier, the Vermunt, comes into view at the end of the valley. The next 2½ km are spent in a pleasant climb to the hut. On the way, two more small glaciers become visible high up on the opposite side of the valley.

At 6½ km is the Wiesbadener Hütte, 2443 meters. Built in 1896, it has been a popular place to stop for a drink and a snack ever since. If you have had enough hiking for the day, the hut is a good turn-around point; if you would like to go on, walk past the hut, take the right fork, and climb toward Radsattel. After a short, steep climb is an intersection. The trail to the right goes to the edge of the Tiroler Glacier and ends. Stay to the left, and follow the red and white paint stripes that mark the trail as it heads straight uphill beside a small stream. After a steep ½ km the

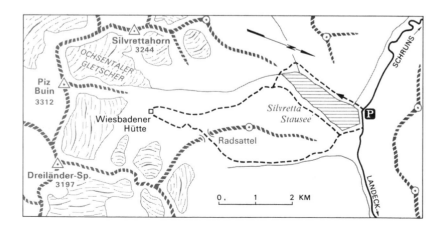

Bieltal (valley) from trail's end at Silvretta-Stausee

trail arrives at a rock-strewn alpine meadow, a great place to sit and soak up the splendid view of the surrounding glaciated peaks.

To complete the loop, continue across the rolling meadow and over the 2701-meter Radsattel, 2½ km from the hut. The trail forks again at the saddle; the left fork continues to the top of Hohes Rad, 2934 meters, while the main trail heads down into the Bieltal.

Views on this side of the pass are pleasant, but not nearly as grand as the ones you left behind. The trail descends steeply for 1 km (snowfields linger here until early August), past a small lake, the Radsee, and then down to a stream on the valley floor. Stay on the right side of the stream and head down the valley, in a gradual but steady descent. At 3½ km from Radsattel, the trail swings around a bend and Silvretta Stausee comes into view.

To complete the loop, walk the east-side trail for 700 meters and then go left along the main road for the final 300 meters back to the start.

69   DARMSTÄDTER HÜTTE

Round trip 20 km, 12½ miles   **Elevation gain 1098 meters,**
Hiking time 7 hours   **3603 feet**
High point 2384 meters, 7820 feet   **Map: Kompaß Wanderkarte 33**

This walk on a service road is as difficult as any hike on a trail. It has steep ascents, fords several small streams, and winds through a muddy pasture before reaching a mountain hut situated in an impressive glacial basin.

The main cross-country autobahn from Bludenz to Innsbruck passes through the mountains, under the famous Arlberg Paß. However, the old road still remains, used by tourists, hikers, skiers, and anyone else who wishes to avoid the high tunnel toll. This road descends 10 km west from the pass to St. Anton am Arlberg, a well-known ski resort town where you will find good beer, *wienerschnitzel,* Austrian atmosphere, and no camping in the entire valley. Near the west entrance to town find the Rendel ski lift below the road on the south side. Descend to the parking lot, elevation 1286 meters.

The hike begins by crossing a wooden bridge. On the far side, find a small "DARMSTÄDTER HÜTTE" sign. Go right. Follow this road, which switchbacks steeply across an open meadow and then heads into trees. Many side roads branch off as you climb out of the valley; however, the way is obvious. For the first kilometer the climb is steep, gaining 300 meters before the road enters a forested side valley. At 2½ km, after a short descent, the road enters open pastureland. This is where the views begin.

The road follows the river, often dry, upvalley, passing over several small streams. At 3½ km a spur road branches off to Tritsch Alpe and Jausenstation Moostal Ski-Hütte. It is possible to cross the river here, walk the next 2 km on trail, and then recross the river on a footbridge and return to the road. After passing the turnoff to Tritsch Alpe the

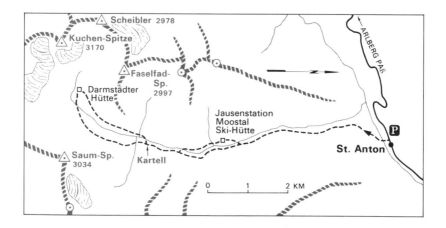

road climbs again, gaining 300 meters while passing through flowered meadows. At 7 km pass Kartell Hütte (a farmhouse), 1974 meters. The views become exciting as the road enters a delightful glacial basin and the Küchel Spitze, Kuchen Spitze, and the idyllic Küchel Glacier come into view.

At 10 km is Darmstädter Hütte, located on a 2384-meter-high green hill with excellent views of the Kuchen Glacier and Scheibler Mountain. From Darmstädter Hütte many trails and hiking routes continue on, higher into the mountains, across glaciers and over passes. Ask the hut-keeper about trail conditions if you decide to continue on.

Moosbach near Darmstädter Hütte

70   RINNENSEE

Round trip 12 km, 7½ miles	**Elevation gain 900 meters,**
Hiking time 5 hours	**2952 feet**
High point 2650 meters, 8692 feet	**Map: Kompaß Wanderkarte 83**

The hike to the high mountain lake called the Rinnensee is delightful, very scenic, and a good workout. The trail—which climbs rapidly through a parklike valley bound on all sides by steep-walled mountains and gleaming glaciers to a hut, the lake, and the summit of a high peak—is very popular.

From Innsbruck travel south toward Brenner Pass. If you are driving, there are two roads to choose from: the A12 autobahn, which is quick and has an expensive toll, and the old Brenner Pass road, Highway 182, which is considerably longer, narrower, and busier. At Schönberg im Stubaital, leave the autobahn, or the highway, and follow Road 183 for 13 km to Neustift. Drive through town, staying on the main road and ig-

View of the Alpeiner Ferner from the Rinnensee Trail

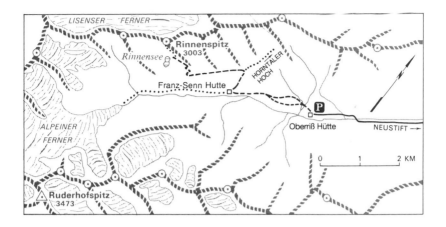

noring all those inviting turnoffs to Ranalt. At 2 km above Neustift, turn right on a narrow, paved road signed to "OBERBERGTAL." Follow this road for 8 km to its end at a large parking lot next to the Oberriß Hütte, elevation 1750 meters.

The trail passes through the courtyard of the hut and then heads across a wide pasture. Shortly after the trail starts to climb, it divides. Both trails go the same place; however, the one on the right is the better maintained. That trail switchbacks steeply over a wooded cliff, levels off, then climbs again to the Franz-Senn Hütte, a large mountain hotel at 2147 meters with a view of the Alpeiner Ferner, located 3 km from the road.

Walk to the front of the hut, cross a wooden bridge, and then turn right at the trail junction and cross a damp meadow. Switchback up a steep hill and cliff to another trail junction. Go left and climb 300 meters up a steep slope to the top of a knoll and a grand viewpoint. The trail levels out for a short breather, then climbs again through a field of huge boulders to the edge of the Rinnensee, 2650 meters.

The marvelous view from Rinnensee of the Ruderhofspitz and glaciers is enough for most people. However, if the day is clear and you have energy to spare, it is worth the effort to continue on to the summit of 3003-meter Rinnenspitz, thus adding an extra 353-meter climb to the day's total. To reach the summit, go back down the trail a few meters from the lake to a junction. Take the trail headed up—up switchbacks, then cables, and, finally, a bit of scrambling—to reach the top. The views go to all points of the compass, with the Lisenser Ferner dominating the scene.

71 STUBAIER ALPEN GLACIER TRAVERSE

One way 17 km, 10½ miles
Hiking time 8 to 10 hours
High point 2676 meters, 8777 feet

Elevation gain 1362 meters,
4467 feet
Map: Kompaß Wanderkarte 83

This traverse of a small section of the Stubaier Alps passes four major glaciers and offers views of many more. The trail is difficult, with long, steep climbs and descents over boulder fields, talus slopes, and rock walls. But the greatest hazard is spending too much time looking at the scenery and not enough time looking at where you are walking.

By car, train, or post bus, travel from Innsbruck to Neustift (see Hike No. 70 for details). In Neustift the road divides; take the right fork and drive to the ski resort at the end of the road. The trail starts here, elevation 1750 meters, or you may ride the lift, if it's running, to the Mittelstation and save 500 meters of climbing.

From the parking lot follow Trail 135, signed "DRESDNER HÜTTE." The trail, which climbs up directly below the lift, is steep, arriving at the 2250-meter Dresdner Hütte and the lift station in just 3 km.

From the hut go east on Trail 102, following signs to "SULZENAU-HÜTTE." The trail switchbacks up a large boulder field to a rib—composed of so many rock needles that, at a distance, it looks feathered—then makes a nerve-wracking ascent over the rib aided by a cable and numerous built-in foot- and handholds. At 1½ km from the hut the trail reaches Peiijoch, 2676 meters, and a magnificent view of the Sulzenauferner with its broad expanse of blue ice splitting into deep crevasses near the snout.

Descending from the pass, the trail follows the thin rim of an old lateral moraine. Two lakes pop into view: Blaue Lacke, fed by snowmelt, and a smaller gray pond, which is glacier-fed. At 7 km from the parking

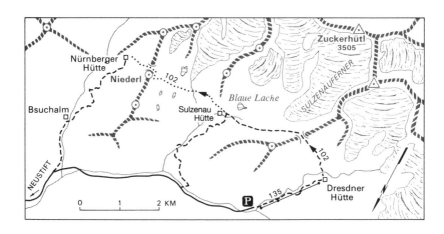

Sulzenauferner (glacier) from Peiljoch

lot, the trail levels for a short distance and then drops to Sulzenau Hütte, 2191 meters. A tired hiker may spend the night or descend to the road on Trail 136.

Trail 102 now heads toward Nürnberger Hütte by climbing, descending, and then climbing again, steeply this time, past several high alpine lakes to a junction.

Stay with Trail 102, climbing up a steep, rocky slope and then over a rock wall with the aid of a cable to reach, at 10 km, Niederl Pass, a sharp 2627-meter ridge marked with a large cross. As it starts down, the trail is steep and difficult, with cables for support. At 11 km the trail arrives at Nürnberger Hütte, 2280 meters, situated in the fourth and final glacial basin. The descent route goes by Besuchalm and reaches the road at 17 km. Ride the bus back up the valley to the parked car or down the valley to other hikes.

72   SCHLEGEISKEES

Round trip 16 km, 10 miles
Hiking time 5 hours
High point 2295 meters, 7528 feet

Elevation gain 395 meters,
1296 feet
Map: Kompaß Wanderkarte 37

The Zillertal Alps south of Innsbruck offer a variety of hiking possibilities and abundant hut facilities, which make it possible to travel for several days with a light pack in a continually changing mountain environment. The Schlegeiskees hike gets you started.

From Innsbruck, head east on the A12 autobahn for 34 km and then south on Highway 169 for 30 km to Mayrhofen. Continue on an expensive toll road, or walk the remaining 7 km of road to Schlegeisspeicher, a large reservoir, elevation 1782 meters.

The hike starts on a service road that parallels the reservoir (marked "TRAIL 502"). It is a scenic walk with ever-changing views as you round the lake. Note: A private taxi may be hired if you do not wish to walk. At 5 km the trail begins, with seemingly endless switchbacks. After each hairpin turn, hikers are rewarded with views of permanent snowfields, icefalls, and crevasses: landmarks of the Austrian–Italian border. At 8 km from the parking lot, the trail arrives at Furtschagl Haus, a hut that hangs on a steep ridge at 2295 meters. This is an excellent place to stretch out and enjoy the commanding view of the Schlegeiskees.

If you have more time, Trail 502 continues for another 35 km. Part of this trail is a *kletterweg* (scramblers' trail), reserved for those who are experienced mountain travelers with a good head for heights. The most difficult section is also the high point of the trail, a 3081-meter pass between the Schönbichler Horn and the Furtschagl Spitz. If you have doubts, turn back.

Beyond the pass, it is up-and-down hiking at high elevation (between

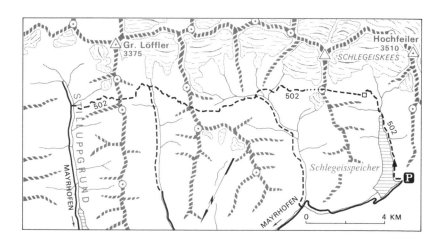

Schlegeiskees (glacier) from Furtschagl Haus

2000 and 2700 meters) until the trail descends to 1500 meters in the Stilluppgrund Valley. Huts along the trail are well placed, never more than an easy day's hike apart. They offer plenty of food, a dry bunk, and Austrian good cheer.

73   SLEEPING GLACIER

Round trip 24 km, 15 miles
Hiking time 10 hours
High point 2796 meters, 9171 feet

Elevation gain 1284 meters,
  4212 feet
Map: Kompaß Wanderkarte 38

The views are grandiose, particularly of the Großglockner massif; and the hut is a splendid place to watch the sun rise on the Schlafenkees, which, literally translated, means sleeping glacier.

View from Alte Prager Hütte

By bus or auto, take Highway 108, which connects Lienz to Mittersill. At 41 km north of Lienz, just before the road enters the toll tunnel, turn west on a road marked "TAUERNHAUS," with a sign advertising a chairlift. Go to the large parking lot at the entrance to town and walk the rest of the way, elevation 1512 meters.

Walk through town and then up a toll road, which is open to auto traffic for 3 hours early in the morning and 2 hours in the evening. The remainder of the day, the road is swarming with hikers. During the first 2 km the road climbs through forest, then levels out into alpine pastures— passing a quaint village, streams, and waterfalls, with glimpses of glaciers—until it ends at 6 km, 1735 meters.

From the end of the road, follow the trail marked "NEUE PRAGER HÜTTE." In a short distance cross a bridge over a torrent and then climb the steep green slope in a series of switchbacks. After gaining 600 meters, the trail approaches the snout of the glacier and the views expand rapidly. At 10 km from Tauernhaus is Alte Prager Hütte, a small hut with refreshments.

For those who wish to go on, the trail continues to climb, crossing rubble fields and snow patches to Neue Prager Hütte, a five-story building 12 km from Tauernhaus, elevation 2796 meters, located between the broad Schlafenkees and the smaller Viltragenkees. If you are planning to spend the night, check in with the hutkeeper and then head outside to take in the glorious views. The smooth, gentle slopes of the glacier tempt exploration; don't try this unless you are equipped with ropes, ice axe, and crampons—and know how to use them. Many crevasses lie hidden underneath those innocent-looking snowfields.

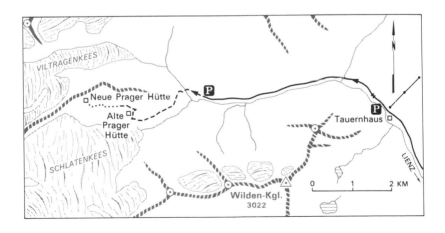

74   FELBERTAUERN TUNNEL OVERPASS

One way 15 km, 9½ miles	Elevation gain 1200 meters,
Hiking time 6½ to 7½ hours	3937 feet
High point 2563 meters, 8407 feet	Map: Kompaß Wanderkarte 38

Felbertauern Tunnel cuts through a range of steep mountains, saving drivers many kilometers and leaving the mountains uncut by roads. While the traffic roars through the tunnel below, hikers enjoy the scenic views, high alpine lakes, meadows, and fresh air on trails over the top.

The hike may be started from the north or south end of the tunnel; however, for purposes of this description, the hike begins from the south end and takes advantage of the higher starting elevation. Follow the road directions for Hike No. 73. From the parking lot at Tauernhaus, elevation 1512 meters, walk through town to the base of the chairlift and then head up through the pasturelands to the top of the lift (or ride up if the chair is running).

At the top of the lift you must pick one of two routes to St. Pöltener Hütte. The shorter route, called the Normalweg, is easy to follow, but badly scarred with power lines and towers. The first 3 km follow a service road, which contours to the next valley and then heads uphill to the hut. This route must be used in early summer when the three lakes route may be covered with snow and hard to follow.

By midsummer, most hikers take the right-hand trail, No. 512, to excellent scenery and three lovely lakes. This route goes up the basin behind the chairlift, passing a T-bar. The trail heads up a steep hill to Grüner See (Green Lake), 2246 meters, where there is a small building and a junction. Continue uphill. The top of the waterfall marks the position of the next lake, the Schwarzer See (Black Lake), 2344 meters. Pass-

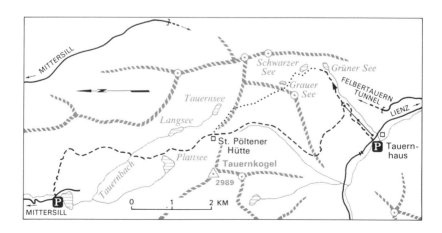

View from Trail No. 512

ing this second lake, the trail follows a cascading river and climbs yet another steep hill and over a loose talus slope to the third colorful lake, the Grauer See (Gray Lake), 2500 meters. Another short climb and the trail reaches Messling-Scharte (Gap), 2563 meters, at 6½ km. The outstanding views of the Venediger Gruppe are an exhilarating distraction as the trail contours down to another gap at 2498 meters. Climb steeply with the aid of cables and then descend to the 2481-meter St. Pöltener Hütte at 8½ km, where the Normalweg and the three lakes route join.

From the hut, follow Trail 917 north, crossing high alpine meadows to Plattsee at 10 km, elevation 2200 meters. The trail drops to cross the Tauernbach above a spectacular waterfall, then makes a short climb before starting the final descent at 12 km. After innumerable switchbacks, the trail arrives at a paved road, 15 km from the start. A short distance beyond is a large parking lot.

To catch the bus, walk down the road 3.7 km to Highway 108. Note: This area is part of the Nationalpark Hohe-Tauern, so no camping is allowed.

75   NEUE REICHENBERGER HÜTTE

Round trip 16 km, 10 miles
Hiking time 8 hours
High point 2586 meters, 8482 feet

Elevation gain 1200 meters,
3936 feet
Map: Kompaß Wanderkarte 46

The tantalizing glimpses of the massive glaciers and high rugged peaks of the Venediger Gruppe provide incentive on this strenuous hike to a high alpine lake and mountain hut. Because it is a long and steep walk, many hikers overnight at the hut, allowing plenty of time for a loop return via Daber Bach or to continue on to St. Jakob the following day.

By bus or by car travel north from Lienz for 28 km on Highway 108 to the town of Matrei in Osttirol. Then go west, following the signs to Prägraten. The road heads up an idyllic valley where views of the 3797-meter Großglockner, the highest mountain in Austria, and neighboring summits are framed by Tirolean villages. Continue past Prägraten to the last bus stop, at Hinterbichl (the bus does occasionally go on—check with the driver). Walk or drive on up the valley the final 1¾ km to a large parking lot (toll) and trailhead, elevation 1403 meters.

The trail begins at the low end of the parking lot, opposite the signed "WC" (public restrooms). Descend a few meters to a farm road, then go right, and cross the river to reach an intersection. Head to the left, following a road 1¾ km to Pebell-alm, a small mountain hut and a couple of restaurants at 1513 meters.

At Pebell-alm the road divides. Go left in front of the hut. In a few meters the very rough-looking trail takes off to the right and heads steeply up beside a waterfall. After gaining 300 meters, the trail switches into a different watershed and continues its steep course, passing Stürmitzer Alm. At 4 km from the parking lot the trail reaches a 2100-meter viewpoint.

For the next 2½ km the trail levels somewhat and contours the hill-

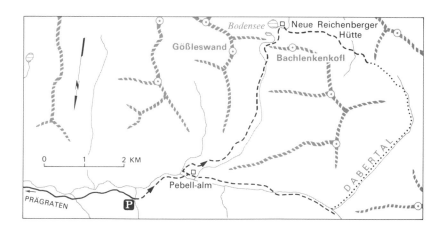

Bodensee and Neue Reichenberger Hütte

side. This respite is followed by a strenuous climb to a divide with dazzling views of glacier-covered mountains. At 8 km the trail arrives at Neue Reichenberger Hütte, 2585 meters, at the edge of the Bodensee, surrounded by green meadows and jagged peaks. If you have time, climb the green slopes of Bachlenkenkofl for fine views of the glacier.

After an overnight stay at the hut, consider an alternative descent via the Dabertal and return to Pebell-alm by the very beautiful waterfall trail. If you do not have to return to your car or pick up your baggage somewhere, head down from the hut through the Trojer Almbach valley to St. Jakob, where you may catch the bus to Lienz.

Maurerbach (river) and Maurerkees (glacier)

76 VENEDIGER GRUPPE

**Round trip to Essener-Rostocker
  Hütte 11 km, 7 miles
Hiking time 4 hours
High point 2208 meters, 7244 feet**

**Elevation gain 805 meters,
  2642 feet
Map: Kompaß Wanderkarte 46**

The Venediger Gruppe are high mountains covered with large, wide glaciers. Views and huts are accessible by trail. All you have to do is hike. With just a couple hours' effort you rise out of the forest and lush meadowlands into fragile subarctic vegetation. Towering above are broad, snowcapped peaks, many with elevations of 3400 meters or more, the flanks of which are covered by unbroken snowfields veiling large glaciers. The open, boulder-strewn slopes below the glaciers tempt the hiker to wander and explore for still better views, hidden peaks, or small lakes.

One of the easiest means of access to the area is the Essener-Rostocker Hütte Trail, which begins near the town of Hinterbichl. If the weather is good and legs and lungs are in shape, you can hut-hop from Essener-Rostocker Hütte to the Johannis Hütte. From there you will find several other fascinating glaciated valleys to explore. Then you can loop back to within a couple of kilometers of your take-off point.

The trail starts from the pay parking lot at Hinterbichl, elevation 1403 meters (see Hike No. 75). Walk to the lower end of the parking lot, pass the restrooms, and descend to a farm road. Walk upvalley and cross the stream to an intersection. Stay right on a gravel road and follow the Maurerbach through lightly wooded forest to Stoanalm, 1450 meters. The trail begins when the service road ends ½ km beyond Stoanalm at the base of a small supply lift.

The climb is steady, up open slopes and across grassy meadows. At 5½ km arrive at the Essener-Rostocker Hütte, 2208 meters. The trail continues beyond the hut to the end of the valley, with views of the sweeping Maurer glaciers. A side trail starting directly above the first bridge beyond the hut leads to two glacial lakes; the upper lake is at the snout of the Malham glacier and the ground is strewn with shiny micaceous rocks rich in small reddish brown garnets.

A rough but well-marked route to Johannis Hütte takes off 1 km above Essener-Rostocker Hütte. The trail, called the Schweriner Weg, crosses a 2800-meter pass and should be hiked only in late summer when the way is free of snow and the weather is clear. From Johannis Hütte the loop route heads downvalley, paralleling the Dorferbach. After 3 km the trail becomes a farm road. Seven km below the hut the road ends at Hinterbichl.

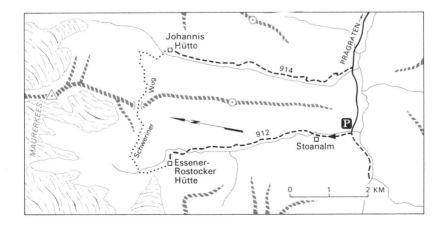

77 LIENZER DOLOMITEN

Round trip to Karlsbader Hütte	Loop trip 18 km, 11¼ miles
7 km, 4½ miles	Hiking time two days
Hiking time 3 hours	High point 2285 meters, 7497 feet
High point 2260 meters, 7415 feet	Elevation gain 665 meters,
Elevation gain 640 meters,	2182 feet
2100 feet	Map: Kompaß Wanderkarte 47

Above green meadowlands rise the high, sharp peaks of the Lienzer Dolomiten range. This area is popular among the international climbing community and, consequently, laced with well-worn trails that lead to the base of every mountain and up every pass. These trails offer enticing opportunities for hiking and roaming.

The classic hike in the Lienzer Dolomiten is a cross-country trip from Oberdrauburg to Hochstadel Haus, over the Hochstadel to Karlsbader Hütte, over another ridge to Kerschbaumer Alm, followed by a climb of Spitzkofel, and ending with a descent to Lienz. This is a great trip, but due to some rather rugged sections where the trail crosses snow slopes and climbs exposed rocks on *kletterwegs* (scrambling routes), that hike is a bit out of the scope of this book. However, the shorter loop from Karlsbader Hütte to Kerschbaumer Alm is ideal for everyone.

For the day hike, drive east from Lienz toward Amlach and Tristach. There is a confusion of roads to be sorted out, but go through Tristach and then head east for 1 km and take the second turn to the right. The paved road goes steeply uphill, passing a turnoff to a campground and Tristacher See. At 3½ km the road is barred by a gate where a toll is paid before you may continue on. If you choose, you may park the car and walk the 4 long km to the road's end and the Lienzer Dolomiten Hütte, elevation 1627 meters.

Walk the service road past the hütte for ½ km to a trail junction. Both

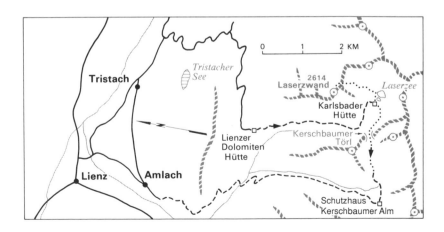

Laserzsee and Karlsbader Hütte

routes lead to Karlsbader Hütte; however, it is best to stay right as the trail on the left is a climbers' route that crosses two peaks before descending to the hut. At 1½ km, pass Instein-Alm, 1669 meters. The path is now near a small stream notable for the way the water suddenly appears from under the gravel in the dry bed. Above this point is a dry channel only used during flood times. At this point you may continue up the service road or take the steeper and considerably more direct trail. Both road and trail climb steadily until reaching Karlsbader Hütte and the adjacent lake, Laserzsee, at 3½ km, 2260 meters.

Hikers planning to do the loop trip should take the bus from Lienz to Lienzer Dolomiten Hütte (check at the Tourist Information office for bus schedules). From Karlsbader Hütte, follow the trail over Kerschbaumer Törl Pass. Descend to Schutzhaus in Kerschbaumer Alm and then head down to the valley floor on Trail 10. At 10 km from the start is an intersection. Follow Trail 10A to Trail 1A. Here you may either walk to Lienz or catch a bus at Amlach.

78   GROßGLOCKNER GLACIER WALK

Round trip 5 km, 3 miles   **Elevation gain 231 meters, 758 feet**
Hiking time 2 hours   **Map: Kompaß Wanderkarte 39**
High point 2600 meters, 8528 feet   **or 50**

Are you planning to climb the Großglockner, or to just gaze at the highest peak in Austria? Either way, this short trail along the Pasterzen Glacier may be one of the highlights of your trip to Austria. This hike allows you to observe the flow and eddies of this active glacier (in some locations the glacier moves as much as 10 centimeters, roughly 4 inches, per day).

The trail is wide enough to accommodate the hordes of people who arrive every day. However, during and after heavy rainstorms or periods of thawing, the trail is closed to protect hikers from falling rocks. Because many of the trails in this region serve mountain climbers as approach routes to the major peaks, there are well-defined trails heading out across the glaciers. No matter how temptingly safe these boot-beaten trails appear, hikers should never cross a glacier unless equipped with climbing gear and the know-how to use it.

Drive the famous Großglockner-Hochalpenstrassen (Highway 107), a toll road between Zell am See and Lienz that passes over the 2575-meter Hochtor Pass. On the south side of the pass, 45 km from Lienz, head northwest for 8 km on the scenic glacier view road, passing the Kaiser Franz-Josephs-Haus, summer home of the Heiligenblut mountaineering school (which specializes in training people to climb the Großglockner), to the parking garage at road's end next to the Freiwandeck, a mountain hotel, restaurant, and souvenir shop, elevation 2445 meters.

The hike begins in a passageway at the far end of the garage and then enters a short tunnel. The trail, blasted into the slabs of glacier-scoured

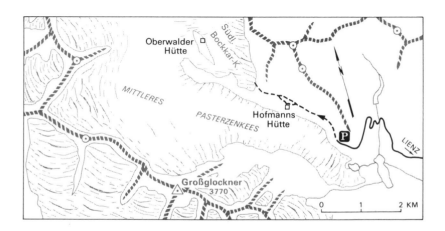

Hofmanns Hütte and Pasterzenkees (glacier)

rock, is wide and smooth, built for the small trucks that supply the mountain huts above. At 1¼ km pass above Hofmanns Hütte, and at 2½ km from the garage reach the road's end at a cascade of water, elevation 2600 meters. From here, a good trail continues another 300 meters to the glacier's edge, where it becomes a climbers' route heading across the glacier to the Oberwalder Hütte.

As noted earlier, unless you are experienced in glacier travel, stop here. For a view, walk 200 meters uphill to the snout of the Südl. Bockkar Glacier and study this moving sea of ice.

79   PINZGAUER SPAZIERGANG

One way 32 km, 20 miles
Hiking time two days
High point 2000 meters, 6560 feet

Elevation gain 800 meters,
2624 feet
Maps: Kompaß Wanderkarte 30
and 38

This is one of the longest and most interesting ridge hikes in the Alps. You walk 32 km from Zell am See to Mittersill, with views to the north of the barren crags along the German–Austrian border, and views to the south of the Glockner massif's vast glaciers. The ridge lies at the edge of timberline and the trail moves from open forest to lush alpine meadows, offering hikers the best of both worlds.

Although this hike is long, it need not be strenuous. The initial elevation can be gained by riding a cable car from Zell am See to the ridgetop. Once on top, the trail is mostly level, contouring around the high points (of course, you may scramble up to any summit you want to). There are no huts near the midway point of this hike; however, numerous trails intersect the ridge route, so it is possible to descend to the valley villages for an overnight stay. Or you can carry a tent and bivouac by a small lake on the north side of the ridge.

From the center of Zell am See, walk, catch a bus, or drive to the base of the Schmittenhöhebahn (cable car), elevation 943 meters. Follow Trail 752 to the top or buy a one-way ticket and ascend to 1865 meters in comfort. From here the ridge walk begins with a steep descent to a 1700-meter saddle that literally bristles with ski lifts. Follow a ski trail west along the ridgetop, but just before reaching the top of the lift (1800 meters), take the trail leading to the left. It traverses the hillside with only very minor ups and downs. At 4 km, pass a ski hut and climb to an elevation of 1900 meters. At 7 km, a trail heads down to Steindorf, where transportation and lodging may be found. At 8 km the trail climbs to a 2000-meter saddle; at 10 km a second trail heads down to Steindorf. Between 11 and 13 km the trail contours steep slopes under the Hochkogel. At 14 and 17 km you pass trails that descend to Uttendorf. At 19 km the

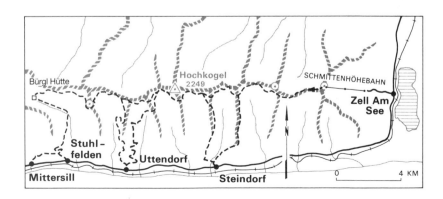

Glockner massif from Pinzgauer Spaziergang Trail

trail crosses below the Pihappenkogel and then drops a little before climbing to a 2000-meter saddle at 23 km. The next kilometer is spent descending to Bürgl Hütte. At this point you may choose to follow the trail over the top of 2363-meter Gießstein, traverse across the basin to Trail 746, and descend to Mittersill; or head down from the hut on a service road to either Stuhlfelden or Mittersill. Once in the valley, take a bus back to Zell am See.

80 MADELZ-KOGEL

Loop trip 19 km, 12 miles
Hiking time 7 hours
High point 2760 meters, 9055 feet

Elevation gain 1312 meters,
  4304 feet
Map: Kompaß Wanderkarte 39

This hike, on the northwest edge of the glaciated Glockner Gruppe, has many variations, from easy to hard. The purest and most strenuous way to enjoy this area is, of course, to hike the entire loop, savoring views that expand with every step. A little less pure, but a lot of fun anyway, is to hike up to the top cable-car station, take a short, free ride on a chairlift gaining an easy 250 meters, and then make the final push to the summit of Madelz-Kogel. Or you may have a lazy day and ride the lifts almost all the way to the top.

The hike begins in the Stubachtal, a highly developed valley. The creeks and streams are dammed, the lakes have been turned into reservoirs, and the hillsides bristle with ski lifts. Yet somehow the glacier-covered peaks that dominate the skyline negate the effect of man's manipulation.

Take the train or drive to Uttendorf, located on Highway 168 just 17 km west of Zell am See or 7 km east of Mittersill. Then catch a bus or drive south, 17 km to road's end at Enzinger Boden, elevation 1448 meters.

If you are not riding all the way to the top, the hike begins from the lower parking lot. Walk past the Seilbahn and follow the signs for Trail 715. Head straight up a steep service road to the first switchback and then continue to parallel the creek on a steep trail. The climb eases as the trail rounds the Grünsee, 1714 meters, to reach the Middle Station of

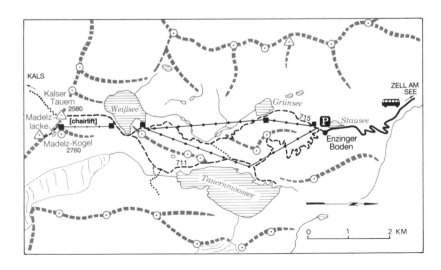

Hiker at the summit of Madelz-Kogel

the Seilbahn at 2 km. Walk around the station and restaurant and follow the trail on a gradual climb through open meadows dotted with glacier-scoured rocks. A trail to Tauernmoossee Reservoir branches off to the left; continue ahead on Trail 715. The Weißsee Reservoir, 2250 meters, is reached at 10 km. Here you may climb the hill to the upper cable car station, the three-story hotel, and the restaurant just for the view, or follow the lakeshore around the hill.

If you have climbed the hill, descend to the chairlift. At the time of this research, the chairlift ride was free, which is a very reasonable price to pay to sit down and let the view unfold around you. If still hiking, follow Trail 517/711 up to the 2580-meter Kalser Tauern and then follow a rough trail southeast up the ridge crest to the 2760-meter summit of Madelz-Kogel. If you came up on the chairlift, walk south past the little Madelzlacke to join the route for the short scramble to the cross on the summit.

If you do not have to return to your car or luggage, continue south from the pass to the town of Kals (Kompaß Wanderkarte 46) and take the bus to Lienz. Before descending, gaze at the surrounding panorama of glaciated summits, dominated by the 3460-meter Ödenwinkelkees.

The loop portion of the hike begins at the base of the chairlift. Go right and follow Trail 711 down an easy series of ladders and cables to Tauernmoossee and hike around the shore of the reservoir on a service road. Just before you reach the Middle Station of the old cable car, go left on an old road, signed as Trail 714, Trail 14, or Trail 4. This overgrown road offers excellent views over the Stubachtal to the Kitzbüheler Alpen as you descend to the parking lot.

81 HUNDSHORN LOOP

Loop trip 14 km, 9 miles
Hiking time 6 hours
High point 1703 meters, 5587 feet

Elevation gain 903 meters,
    2963 feet
Map: Kompaß Wanderkarte 13

With a 360-degree view of magnificent peaks, valleys, villages, farms, and forests—and an 80-meter-high waterfall thrown in for good measure—the loop trip around, and to the summit of, the 1703-meter-high Hundshorn is a great hike.

From the junction of Highways 321 and 311 at the outskirts of the resort city of Lofer near the Austrian–German border, travel south on Highway 311 for 200 meters and then turn east on a road signed "SCHEFFSNOTH." Cross a concrete bridge to an intersection, turn left for 400 meters to a water trough in the village of Scheffsnoth, and then turn right. At the next intersection, go left and follow the signs to Knappenftadl for 2.4 km. The road ends at a restaurant. Park here, elevation 800 meters.

The trail begins above the parking lot on a gated forest road and is marked with a lengthy sign that lists, among other names, "JOCHING ALM, SCHEFFSNOTHER," and "HUNDS ALM." After the road switchbacks around an old gravel pit, find the trail on the right. There is a short climb, then Trail 25 joins from the right. Continue up to the 1026-meter Kematstein Alm, reached at 1 km. The trail levels off and contours around a small but deep valley at the head of which is a waterfall that plunges 80 meters.

At 1¾ km is the second of many junctions, this one with Trail 25B to Jochingalm, the return route for the loop. Keep to the right, first walking on the level and then climbing. Your reward will be a beautiful little glade with heather, trees, and a small bubbling brook. The trail crosses the brook and climbs to Scheffsnoth Alm at 1354 meters. Once in the

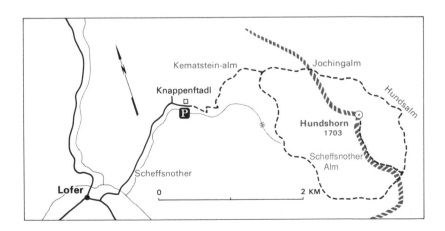

Reiter Alpe from near the summit of the Hundshorn

alm, the trail is hard to find. Head for the nearest building and then follow the painted stakes across the pasture. Just beyond the highest farm building is another intersection. Go left on Trail 24, heading up the valley to a 1450-meter saddle. From the saddle, go left on Trail 24A, for a 1-km climb to the top of Hundshorn where the views include the Reiter Alpe, the glacier-covered Großglockner massif, and the icy Dochsteins.

Back at the saddle, the trail continues north, dropping to Hundsalm and then down to a 1323-meter saddle and a four-way trail junction. Take Trail 24, marked "JOCHING ALM," which climbs a little and then drops as it contours under the steep wooded hillside below the Hundshorn. The Joching Alm is reached at about 9½ km, elevation 1300 meters. Go to the lowest point and take the left-hand trail, No 25B, which drops in a series of short switchbacks into a steep gully. There, near Kematstein Alm, the loop ends. Go right and descend back to the trailhead at the Knappenftadl restaurant.

82   LOFERER STEINBERGE

Round trip 9 km, 5½ miles
Hiking time 6 hours
High point 1996 meters, 6547 feet
Elevation gain 1196 meters,
**   3923 feet**
Map: Kompaß Wanderkarte 13

Leopard's bane

The stone mountains of Lofer are well named. They rise out of timber-covered hills to dominate the valleys and villages below. All trails into the area are very steep, gaining considerable elevation in a relatively short distance. Above the barrierlike cliffs that surround the Loferer Steinberge, the going is easier and the hiker may explore the cirques and meadows on well-marked routes.

From the town of Lofer, near the Austrian–German border, the trail is best accessed by car or taxi. Starting from the intersection of Highways 312 and 311 at the southern end of town, follow Highway 312 for 1.3 km toward Innsbruck. Turn left, opposite the bus stop, onto a nameless road marked with a sign to Schmidt-Zabierow Hütte. Drive 2 km up the paved road, staying right at the only intersection to avoid the army camp. The road ends at a parking lot, elevation 880 meters.

Following signs for Schmidt-Zabierow Hütte and a line of red paint dots, head up Trail 601. The trail stays on the valley floor to the base of the cliffs at the end of the valley; then, without further ado, the trail switchbacks up through forest, then meadows, and then over a series of

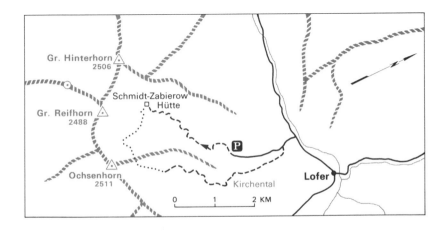

Schmidt-Zabierow Hütte

giant steps. The map names three steps: Unter, Mittleres, and Oberes Tret (lower, middle, and upper); however, when hiking there seems to be many more. Toward the top, the vegetation gives way to weathered limestone. The trail weaves its way through rocky slabs and up a small knoll to the hut, 1966 meters, set in a large cirque.

Weather and time permitting, let ambition dictate your route through the cirques, or make a loop trip by following Trail 613 to Ochsenhorn and Kirchental. This steep, rocky, and often slippery trail is challenging and full of interest. Follow the double red stripes over several ridges and pass two trail junctions. The third junction is the Ochsenhorn Trail, marked with a red stripe. Go left to descend to the valley, or right to climb the Ochsenhorn. If heading to the valley, a bit of easy scrambling down the steep slope leads to the head of the valley. Farther down is a large church, which may provide a clue to the origin of the name Kirchental. Walk past the church and go left on a trail that heads back toward Lofer, intersecting the road to the hut 1.6 km below the parking area.

83   TRAUNSTEIN

Round trip 12 km, 7½ miles
Hiking time 7 hours
High point 1691 meters, 5548 feet

Elevation gain 1267 meters,
  4157 feet
Map: Freytag & Berndt
  Wanderkarten 284

Traunstein is a solitary peak that stands guard over the east side of the
Traun Gmundner See. The view from the summit is extraordinary, with
panoramic coverage of the rolling hills to the north, east, and west, and
to the Höllengebirge, Totes Gebirge, and the glacier-covered Dachstein
group to the south.

Three very difficult trails climb to the summit of the Traunstein. Two
of the trails are rock-scramblers' routes that weave their way up through
the cliffs with the aid of cables and ladders. The third trail to the summit
is for experienced hikers who have a good head for heights and a lot of energy to tackle the rough trail, which is steep and climbs over bands of
limestone cliffs with occasional assistance from a cable.

To reach the trailhead, turn off the A1 autobahn 46 km west of Linz at
the Steyermühl exit. Follow Road 144 south 12 km to Gmunden. Turn
left just before Road 144 reaches the lake and drive along the east shore
for 5.7 km to a parking lot at the end of the official road, elevation 424
meters. Gmunden may also be reached by train or bus.

Begin the hike from the east side of the parking lot and head south on
a well-maintained, restricted-entry road signed "MAIR ALM HÜTTE." The

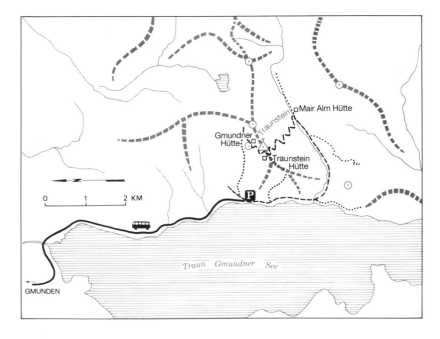

Hiker near the summit of the Traunstein

road starts off by paralleling the lakeshore. At 1 km pass through two tunnels and then cross a high bridge over a narrow gorge. The road then heads steeply up a narrow valley to reach, at 3½ km, a small picnic area on the left, which marks the start of the trail. Leave the road here and begin the long, hard grind up the remaining 2½ km to the summit ridge.

As the trail crests the low end of the summit, two huts come into view. On the left is the Naturfreunde Hütte, a private facility. Follow the trail to the right and climb past the Gmundner Hütte to reach the large cross that marks the 1691-meter summit pyramid. Enjoy the view, but don't linger. The descent takes nearly as long as the climb.

If you choose one of the two rock-scrambling routes to the summit, be prepared to scramble up steep slopes on rocks that are slippery when wet. If uncertain of your abilities but determined to try one of these trails, carry a climbing harness, two slings, and a couple of carabiners so you may clip on to the cables as needed. It is advised to descend via the Mair Alm Trail. To reach the Gmundner Hütte Trail, follow the road that goes uphill to the left from the parking lot. Look for the start of the trail on your right in ½ km. The Naturfreundsteig begins 1 km up the road toward Mair Alm and is the more difficult of the two.

Alpine hut at Prielschutzhaus

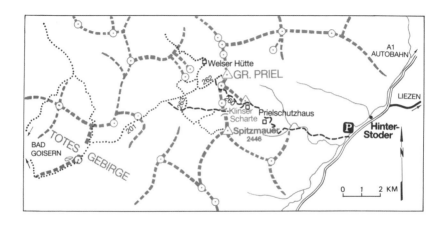

84 TOTES GEBIRGE

Round trip 32 km, 20 miles
Hiking time two to three days
High point 2446 meters, 8025 feet

Elevation gain 1841 meters,
6040 feet
Map: Kompaß Wanderkarte 68
and 69

Totes Gebirge, the Dead Mountains, are a beautiful range of limestone summits encircling a high plateau that supports little to no vegetation, hence the name. The lack of vegetation allows for a near-endless parade of open vistas that makes this scenic area inviting for hiking, wandering, and scrambling on the many trails and *klettersteigs* (secured climbing routes). A day hike will only bring you to the edge of the range, so it is best to plan several days here.

This hike is an introduction to the eastern end of the Totes Gebirge. Once in the range, opportunities are many for loop trips, traverses, or climbs to the high summits. Because the snow lingers in the passes on the steep hillsides through much of the summer, it is best to plan your visit for late August or September.

The Prielschutzhaus at timberline is a convenient, though expensive, base camp for exploration into the range. Before you set out, check with the Tourist Information office at Hinterstoder to be sure the hut is open. If tenting, you have to stop in the meadows below the hut; there is no reliable source of water above.

The hike begins near Hinterstoder, reached by following Highway 138 for 23 km north from Liezen or 58 km south from the A1 autobahn. In either case, turn off Highway 138 and head west for 13 km to Hinterstoder, and then continue on for another 600 meters to find a large parking area on the right side of the road, elevation 605 meters.

Cross the bridge and head up a farm road marked variously as Trail 201, 04, or 01. Also seen are signs for Trails 9, 10, and 11, which wander along with the main trail for a spell. Keep a watch for signs to "PRIELSCHUTZHAUS," which are much more informative than the trail numbers.

Pass a small lake with views of the Spitzmauer and the Gr. Priel and, shortly beyond, leave the road for a 500-meter section of trail; then rejoin the road. After 2 km of valley rambling, the road crosses a bridge and ends. Head up, out of the valley, on a rough and slippery trail that ascends rapidly, passing several waterfalls before reaching the 1420-meter Prielschutzhaus at 6 km.

Above the hut, Trail 201 climbs to a narrow pass, the Klinser Scharte, and then traverses the entire range to Bad Goisern (near Bad Ischl). A little more accessible is the hike to the Welser Hütte, where you may use Trails 260, 262, 263, and 201 to make a loop around a small portion of this rugged plateau. For hikers with a good head for heights and some rock-climbing experience, the *klettersteig* (scramblers' route) up 2446-meter Spitzmauer is a good day trip from the hut. Although the route is protected by cables, it is recommended to carry climbing harness, slings, and carabiners with you.

85 GESÄUSE MOUNTAINS

Round trip 10 km, 6½ miles
Hiking time 4 hours
High point 1687 meters, 5538 feet

Elevation gain 836 meters,
2743 feet
Map: Freytag & Berndt
Wanderkarten 6

Trails to beautiful meadows, trails to sweeping views, trails to high mountain summits—in other words, trails for every taste. The hike described here takes you from the valley, through forest and meadows, to Heß Hütte, where you may choose a rough trail up 2191-meter Zinödl for views over the Gesäuse to the Großer Buchstein, follow a *kletter* (scramblers') route up the 2117-meter Planspitze for more views, take a very challenging *kletter* route to the 2365-meter summit of Hochtor with your climbing gear in reserve in your pack, or wander the hills near the hut looking for chamois.

From Liezen, follow Highway 138 east along the Enns River. After 21 km pass through Admont and enter the Gesäuse where the valley narrows, becoming a deep gorge cut through the mountains. Continue east on Highway 146 for another 10 km and then go right, following the signs to Johnsbach. Head up this road for 8 km, passing through the small town to reach the well-signed trailhead, elevation 851 meters. If traveling on the train, disembark at the Johnsbach Station in the Enns Valley and ride the post bus, call a mountain taxi, or hike up to the trailhead.

The trail, signed No. 601 or, occasionally, No. 1, begins as a road and immediately narrows as it crosses a muddy cow pasture. Then it's into the woods for the long climb to the high meadows. If planning to camp, stop in the meadows well below Heß Hütte where there is an as-

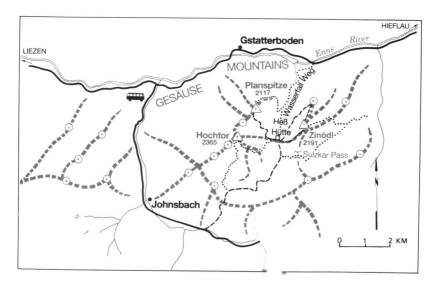

Farm buildings and Hochtor (peak)

sured source of water, or head east over Sulzkar Pass to the spring on the other side.

Heß Hütte, 1687 meters, is reached at 5½ km. From there you will find trails taking off in all directions, including one trail that heads down to the Enns Valley, called the Wasserfallweg, which makes its scenic descent with the aid of cables and ladders. However, for the best views head up—the Panoramaweg is exceptionally scenic and worth the hike even if you were not planning to go to the summit of Zinödl.

Trail up the Bärenschützklamm

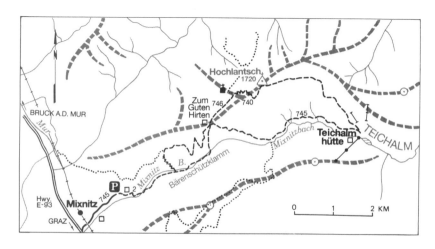

86   BÄRENSCHÜTZKLAMM

Loop trip 19 km, 12 miles
Hiking time 7 hours
High point 1720 meters, 5643 feet

Elevation gain 1227 meters,
4026 feet
Map: Freytag & Berndt 131

The objective of this hike is the Hochlantsch, a peak of gleaming white limestone with an all-encompassing view over the rolling green hills that comprise the easternmost reaches of the Alps. But getting there is more than half the fun of this hike. The trail climbs through the Bärenschützklamm, a deep gorge on the Mixnitzbach. The hike up the gorge is accomplished with the aid of 160 ladders and bridges that are suspended from the cliff walls, often hanging over the foaming torrent. After the gorge the trail becomes a normal path through the woods and meadows, but the fun is not over. Ibex inhabit this area and, if you are lucky, may be seen scratching themselves with their long curved horns or butting heads. Plan a little extra hiking time to allow for lingering on the way.

The hike begins at Mixnitz, located 2 hours south of Vienna between Graz and Bruck a.d. Mur on Highway E93. If driving, turn off the highway 13.5 km south of Bruck a.d. Mur and go east, crossing the Mur River. Drive under the railroad tracks and then turn right and follow the signs to Bärenschützklamm on a narrow road that winds past several *gasthofs* and then heads out through the fields. After 1.4 km the road ends at a parking area, elevation 492 meters. If arriving by train, call a taxi or walk south from the *bahnhof* and follow the signs.

The trail starts from the upper parking lot. Walk pass the small bistro (a small map of the area may be purchased here) and head upvalley on a wide and rocky trail. Ignore all side trails and stay on the main path, which is well marked with paint. After 1½ km the trail divides; stay right on Trail 745 (you will return on the left-hand trail, No. 2). Shortly beyond is a tollhouse where a modest fee is paid before entering the Bärenschützklamm.

At the top of the gorge the trail makes a short climb through the forest to reach Zum Guten Hirten, a small restaurant that marks the first possible turn-around point. From the restaurant, head uphill on Trail 746. At 5 km from the parking lot, this trail ends at an intersection. To the left, Trail 740 crosses the balcony of a second restaurant and then descends 20 meters to St. Jacobs, a little church perched on the cliff. The route to the summit goes right on Trail 740, climbing a rough and slippery hillside to the 1720-meter summit of the Hochlantsch and a large cross.

If you would like to turn your descent into a loop, go east from the summit through forest and meadows, crossing several roads to reach the resort community of Teichalm at 9 km. Just before the first *gasthaus* (hotel), turn right on Trail 745 and follow it for 6 km down the Mixnitzbach, back to Zum Guten Hirten. For the final descent, it is better to avoid the ladder trail and a second toll by following Trail 746 down the hill. At 17 km turn left on Trail 2 and follow it back to Trail 745 for the final leg of the loop.

AUSTRIA
Vienna

87   THE SCHNEEBERG

Round trip 24 km, 15 miles
Hiking time 10 hours
High point 2076 meters, 6811 feet

Elevation gain 1491 meters,
4892 feet
Map: Freytag & Berndt 022

The Schneeberg is the highest mountain in the eastern Alps. This rugged limestone peak is located just 1½ hours from central Vienna and is an extremely popular destination during the summer.

The hike described below is the most popular of the many routes up the mountain, beginning in Puchberg am Schneeberg and climbing, by the easiest trail, to the highest summit of the Schneeberg. However, there is a way to circumvent the long climb, by riding the historic 100-year-old cog railroad for the first 9 km up the mountain. This allows hikers a couple of extra hours to enjoy the fabulous views from the high plateau near the summit. If choosing to ascend by the train, the hike is only 15 km long with a 281-meter elevation gain.

From Vienna, head south 43 km on the A2 autobahn to Wr. Neustadt and then go west on Road 26 for 28 km to "PUCHBERG A. SCHN." Park near the *bahnhof* (train station), elevation 585 meters. To reach this area by train, take the Südbahn from Vienna.

The *bahnhof* is where you must decide whether you will ride or walk up the mountain. On the weekends there may be a several-hour wait for the train, so you might as well walk. From the train station, head up through town to a major intersection, go right, then left, and parallel the cog railroad up the hill. The trail follows a wide service road for the first 7½ km to Baumgartner Hütte, 1397 meters. The train stops here to tank

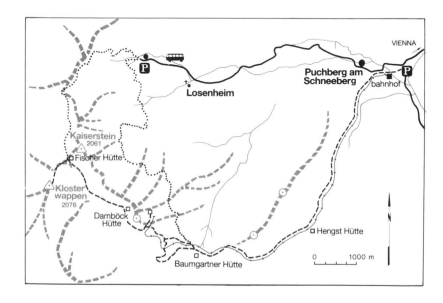

204

Cog railroad at Baumgartner Hütte

up on water for the final push to the top. Most passengers buy huge jam- or cheese-filled pastries at the restaurant.

Beyond the hut, the trail descends briefly and then climbs to an intersection. Follow either the trail marked with yellow—steep, rough, and very direct—or the trail marked with green—a longer, more gradual ascent. A third trail, marked with red, traverses north around the flanks of the mountain to Losenheim.

At 9 km (by the yellow trail) is the railroad terminal station, 1792 meters. Facilities here include a hut, a restaurant, and a small church with an excellent view. Follow the wide, well-marked trail from the restaurant to Damböck Hütte and then continue on to Fischer Hütte. Climb over the Kaiserstein, 2061 meters, for a panoramic view of the Pre-Alps, and then go southwest on the open summit ridge to Klosterwappen, 2076 meters, for a view of the Raxalpe area and the Höllental. For the surefooted, a rough trail completes the summit triangle and then descends back to the main trail ½ km above Damböck Hütte.

Several alternate descents are possible. From the summit, hikers may head north along a ridge crest to Losenheim and take the bus or taxi back to Puchberg am Schneeberg. This is not recommended in poor weather when the winds howl over the exposed ridge and the limestone rocks are slippery underfoot.

If looking for further hiking in this area, the nearby Raxalpe is a scenic and challenging area. Reichenau serves as a hiking center with trailheads located in the Höllental. This is also a popular rock-climbing area.

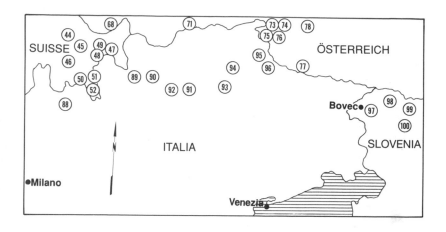

NORTHEASTERN ITALY

T he Alps of Northeastern Italy present an amazing contrast to the snow- and ice-carved summits of France and Switzerland. These mountains, known as the Dolomites, were formed from coral rocks, uplifted from the ocean and ingrained with calcite. The landscape took shape during an ice age when the force of the glaciers carved the major valleys. Erosion denuded the isolated hills and then wind and rain sculpted them into jagged towers that, in turn, splintered into needles and pinnacles. The cliffs and hills vary in color from white to rose, creating an incredibly beautiful scene that has captured the imaginations of hikers from around the world.

The Dolomites lie on the southern edge of the Alps, protected from the cold winds of the north. Days are frequently sunny and often warm. Because of the excellent climate, this is a popular hiking area. Campgrounds, trails, and huts are very crowded in July and August. The best time to visit this area is in September, when summer vacations are over and the trails are still snow-free.

The Italian Dolomites are also known as the Southern Tirol. This area was part of Austria until the peace agreements at the end of World War I awarded it to Italy. Because nationalistic feelings still run strong, place names on maps are printed in two languages, and the inhabitants speak three: Italian, German, and the local Ladin. This makes for some difficulty when traveling in the Dolomites, as fewer of the local inhabitants are likely to speak English than in other parts of Europe. (Proficiency in three languages is considered to be enough.) Be sure to carry an Italian road map, because any road map of Austria that extends into the Dolo-

Lago di Nambino, the Brenta Dolomites in distance (Hike No. 92)

mite region will give the names in German, leaving you hopelessly confused at road signs.

Whatever language you see or hear, the Italian Dolomites provide some of the best hiking and friendliest atmosphere in the Alps. The mixture of jovial Tiroleans and exuberant Italians creates an ambience of noisy trails and huts with much laughter and good-natured fun.

88   SENTIERO ROMA

Loop trip 36 km, 22½ miles
Hiking time three days
High point 2765 meters, 9069 feet

Elevation gain 5400 meters,
17,712 feet (cumulative)
Maps: Kompaß Wanderkarte 92
and 93

On the sunny side of the Bregaglia Alps, a rugged trail—the Sentiero Roma—makes a fascinating and challenging open-ended loop over cirques and steep ribs at the head of Val Masino. The views on this loop are exciting, with the Alps rising above in massive granite cliffs, sharp pinnacles, and small glaciers.

The Sentiero is a hike for experienced hikers only. This difficult trail is poorly marked and hikers find themselves scrambling over boulder fields and working their way across (or around) ice-hard patches of snow. The seven passes along the route vary from easy to difficult, some requiring the strategically placed steel cables for handholds and iron spikes for footholds. However, for anyone who decides to leave the loop early, there are several alternate trails that descend to the valley.

The complete loop takes three full days. Three refuges along the way serve meals and offer shelter. In addition, hikers may use the two unattended bivouac huts. The loop may be walked in either direction, but most people start at Bagni del Masino, the highest point on the loop accessible by road. At the end of the loop, a bus may be taken back up the valley from Cataeggio, avoiding a long road walk to retrieve your car.

Drive or take public transportation to the Lago di Como near the Italian—Swiss border. From the east side of the lake, go east on highway 38 for 21 km to Stne. di Ardenno-Masino. Head north on road 404 for 18 km to Bagni del Masino, where the hike begins.

If you prefer to simply sample this area, consider a 5-hour trek to Rifugio Allievi, the midpoint of the Sentiero Roma. The hike starts off in

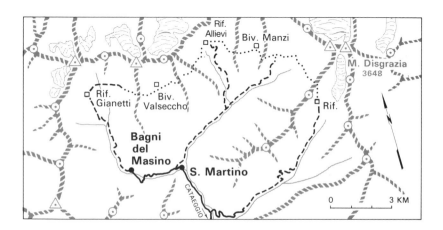

Fog-covered peaks near Rifugio Allievi

the farmlands and climbs through forest to meadows and onto barren rock and snow. To reach the trailhead, drive or take the bus to San Martino, elevation 923 meters. Head up the Valle di Mello on a rough road that is better to walk than to drive. At 4 km the road turns into trail, crosses several farmyards, and then leaves the valley floor. Near 5 km the trail divides; stay left, climbing steadily up to reach the 2385-meter Rifugio Allievi at 10 km.

König-Spitz and Suldenferner (glacier)

89 HINTER SCHÖNECK
(Stelvio National Park)

Round trip 14 km, 9 miles
Hiking time 6 hours
High point 3128 meters, 10,260 feet

Elevation gain 1300 meters,
 4264 feet
Map: Kompaß Wanderkarte 52

Climb Hinter Schöneck, a 3128-meter summit, to a breathtaking panorama of glaciers, mountains, and valleys in Stelvio National Park. For an added incentive, if needed, this is not a heavily hiked trail!

By post bus or auto, travel to the town of Sponding on Highway 40, between Reschenpass on the Austrian border and Merano (also called Meran). At Sponding, head south on Highway 38 for 9 km to Gomago and then go left on a paved road signed "SOLDA/SULDEN." Follow this road, staying on the west side of the valley when the road splits, to Solda-Sulden (the lower end of town is also called St. Gertraud). Once in town, follow the main road east, across the Suldenbach, and then head uphill to find the trailhead on the left, opposite the Hotel Post Zum Ortler, elevation 1850 meters.

Take Trail 6 uphill 100 meters to Hotel Merlet. At the far side of the hotel, turn left on Trail 19, a wide service road that climbs through the forest. At 2 km Trail 18 joins Trail 19; continue up the road. At 2½ km is timberline and Stieralm, 2248 meters. Just beyond the first building, locate a trail heading up through the meadows, marked with yellow stripes painted on rocks. Many of the rocks are set on end, and in places where the trail disappears only the rocks and yellow marks indicate the way.

The trail heads up open meadows to a shoulder of Vorder Schöneck. The top of this 2908-meter peak is bypassed and the trail contours along the ridge crest to Hinter Schöneck. Continue on the trail through the rubble and flower fields to the 3128-meter summit, 7 km from the trailhead, and enjoy the views of glaciated peaks to the east and south and of the 3905-meter Ortler peak to the west.

If you are surefooted, this hike may be turned into a loop with a short 3-meter section of rock scrambling about 200 meters below the summit. To do the loop, continue to follow the yellow markers to a saddle a short way beyond the summit and then head down over the rubble. In 2 km reach Düsseldorfer Hütte (Rifugio Serristori) at 2727 meters. Head down from the hut to an intersection and then follow Trail 5 through meadows, paralleling the Zaybach back to the Hotel Merlet.

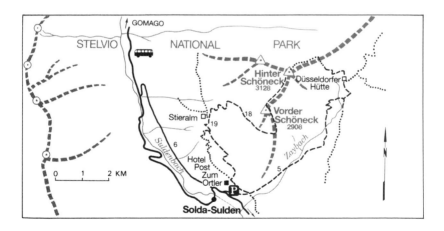

90 RIFUGIO G. PAYER
(Stelvio National Park)

One way to Trafoi 10½ km,
6½ miles
Hiking time 6 hours
High point 3020 meters, 9906 feet

Elevation gain 1170 meters,
3838 feet
Map: Kompaß Wanderkarte 52

The Ortler Gruppe are high, glacier-covered peaks in Stelvio National
Park near the Swiss–Italian border. The highest peak is the 3905-meter
Ortler. Below its summit is the Rifugio G. Payer, perched on a razor-
sharp ridge at 3020 meters, a popular hut for hikers and climbers alike.
Views from the hut are extraordinary.

Bus and auto directions are the same as those for Hinter Schöneck
(Hike No. 89). Near the entrance to Solda-Sulden find Pension Bambi on
the right and park in the large lot behind, elevation 1850 meters.

Several trails begin just above the parking lot. Follow Trail 4, which,
at first, is also Trail 8. The trail soon divides; continue uphill on Trail 4.
After ½ km, pass a junction with Trail 21 and at 1½ km pass a junction
with Trail 13. Trail 4 continues uphill through thinning forest and then
enters an open meadow with a large talus slope on the right and Mount
Ortler towering overhead. Up and to the right is Tabaretta Hütte.

After passing a couple more junctions, the trail reaches Tabaretta
Hütte, 2536 meters, 4 km from the parking lot. From here on, the way to
Rifugio G. Payer is narrow and often steep, traversing several slide
areas. At 2877 meters the trail crosses a high pass with an excellent view
of the 48 switchbacks on the road to Stelvio Pass. At 5½ km arrive at the
3020-meter-high Rifugio G. Payer.

If transportation can be arranged, descend to Trafoi, a small village on
the Stelvio Pass road and the birthplace of the famous Italian skier Gus-

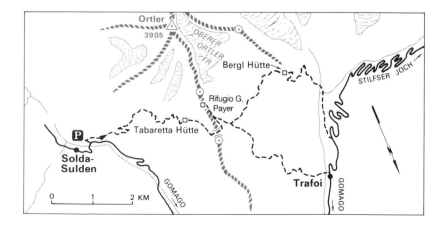

Rifugio G. Payer on left, Ortler (mountain) center

tavo Thoeni. The trail to Trafoi takes off below the final ascent to Rifugio G. Payer, and switchbacks down through boulders and talus. After descending 500 meters, pass the poorly marked Trail 18 on the left leading to Bergl Hütte (also called Rifugio A. Borletti). (Trail 18 crosses several large snowfields and should not be attempted unless you verified beforehand that it is in good condition.)

The main trail continues to the right, passing a service lift and an abandoned hut at 1½ km that marks the beginning of a wide road/trail. At 4½ km is the beginning of a confusion of crisscrossing trails. Head down in as straight a line as possible to the Trafoierbach and then climb a short hill to Trafoi, 1543 meters, 5 km from Rifugio G. Payer.

91   DOLOMITI DI BRENTA

Round trip to Rifugio Brentéi
12 km, 7½ miles
Hiking time 4½ hours
High point 2120 meters, 6954 feet

Elevation gain 600 meters,
1968 feet
Map: Kompaß Wanderkarte 073

Located on the western end of the Dolomites, the Brenta massif is endowed with a beauty all its own. Perhaps this is because these mountains are altered coral reefs that were pushed up from the sea millions of years ago. Unlike many summits in the Swiss and French Alps, Dolomite summits are often rounded. The rock is softer and has a reddish gray color.

In the Brenta massif, the hiking is quite varied, with trails to suit all tastes and endless views no matter where you go. Easy day hikes follow wide trails with an occasional tunnel or handrail. On sunny weekends, thousands of hikers—from children carried in backpacks to grandmothers in long dresses accompanied by teenage girls in bikinis—may be seen on the easier trails. The difficult trails go along high ledges with cables for holding on to and should only be attempted by hikers with a good head for heights. Often, steps have been cut for feet, or steel footholds and handholds have been sunk into the rock. Steel ladders, tunnels, and bridges are common. On the more difficult trails it is best to carry a seat harness, slings, and carabiners; a hard hat is recommended. Do your exploring in August when the snow has melted from the steep gullies; otherwise, stick to the lower trails.

Below Brenner Pass on the Italian–Austrian border is the town of Bolzano (also called Bozen). At 37 km south of Bolzano, on the road to Trento, find Road 43 and follow it north 28 km to join Road 42. Head southwest another 22 km to Dimaro and then go south on Road 239 for 19 km climbing to Madonna di Campiglio. Drive to the south end of town, turn sharply left at a poorly marked intersection, and cross a bridge to reach a confusing intersection. Follow the middle road, signed "RIFUGIO

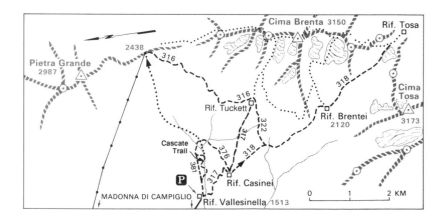

Mountain chapel in the Dolomiti di Brenta

CASCATE," which bears right. When the road divides in 500 meters, stay left and follow it 3.2 km (mostly on dirt) to road's end and a large parking lot at the Rifugio Vallesinella, elevation 1513 meters.

The first destination is Rifugio Casinei, which can be reached by three trails of varying difficulty. Trail 317 is only 1½ km long and very direct. Trail 381, in combination with 376, is twice as long and has an easy grade. In the middle is the third route, which climbs by the Cascate, a somewhat challenging trail, passing between three waterfalls that pop directly out of a rock wall.

From Rifugio Casinei, follow the wide and well-graded Trail 318 for the next 3 km. The trail climbs steeply at first, then contours around hillsides, follows ledges, and passes through a tunnel before reaching Rifugio Brentei, 2120 meters.

The same trail continues another 2 km and then becomes a scramble route over rock to Rifugio Tosa and various loop trips. Or you may try some of the cable routes. For example, the Via delle Bocchette Trail, which begins a short distance above the Rifugio Brentei, is a cable route of medium difficulty that traverses the face of a cliff. For more details on cable routes, read the Sierra Club totebook, *Huts and Hikes in the Dolomites,* by Ruth Rudner.

92   THE FIVE LAKES LOOP

Loop trip 14 km, 8½ miles
Hiking time 5 hours
High point 2400 meters, 7872 feet

Elevation gain 750 meters,
** 2460 feet**
Map: Kompaß Wanderkarte 73

For a perspective of the Brenta Dolomites completely different from Hike No. 91, explore the mountains west of Madonna di Campiglio. Here you will find views of the entire Brenta Group, from the magnificent needles to snowcapped peaks. You will also see the striking contrast between the rock of the Brentas, which is dolomite, and these western mountains, which are composed of a form of granite. Even more striking is the water. In the Brenta, the water disappears into underground channels; in the western mountains, the water runs on the surface in numerous streams and, thanks to the scooping effect of ancient glaciers, many lakes are formed. It is these lakes that distinguish this hike.

The hike begins just north the town of Madonna di Campiglio (see directions for Hike No. 91). Leave Road 239 at 1.6 km south of Passo Campo Carlo Magno, go right on a road marked Val Nambino, and drive 700 meters to a junction. Park here, elevation 1650 meters.

Start the hike by walking the right-hand fork from the intersection to road's end, then head up the eroded trail for 1½ km to Lago di Nambino. This little lake is surrounded by forest and meadows; many tourists come for the view and for snacks at the restaurant.

Near the outlet of the lake, keep right to an intersection and go left on Trail 266, signed "MAGA BUCA DEI CAVALLI," which climbs high above Lago di Nambino. With a series of short switchbacks the trail reaches the meadows where the track is sketchy. The trail divides several times; stay left, following the signs to "LAGO NERO" painted on the rocks. The trail descends slightly to Lago Nero and then climbs to Lago Serodoli di Sopra, 3270 meters. If time allows, wander around the lake to the neighboring

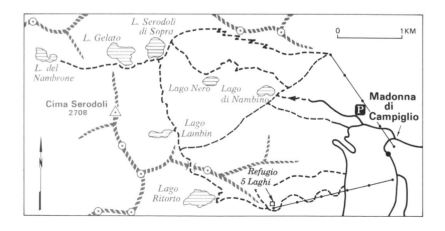

Lago di Nambino, the Brenta Dolomites in distance

Lago Gelato and several smaller ponds and, if time allows, take a side trip to beautiful Lago del Nambrone.

To continue the loop, cross the outlet of Lago Serodoli di Sopra and follow the well-marked trail contouring south, up and down, to Lago Lambin. From here continue south over a low pass and drop down to Lago Ritorto at 8 km, 2053 meters. Follow the broad path to Rifugio 5 Laghi at the top of a ski lift and then descend on the wide service road to a larger road. Go left and walk on pavement for the final 500 meters back to the starting point. (It is possible to follow an obscure trail from the top of the ski lift to the paved road. This trail begins on the left side of the buildings and climbs around the open basin before descending.)

93   SELLA DOLOMITES

One way 7 km, 4½ miles
Hiking time 3 hours
High point 2260 meters, 7413 feet

Elevation gain 100 meters, 328 feet
Map: Kompaß Wanderkarte 59

To sample the Sella Group and its outstanding views, try this downhill route at the foot of the cliffs. On the way are close-up views of two climbing routes and a waterfall. Since this is a one-way hike, it is best to take a bus from the city of Corvara to Passo Gardena, elevation 2137 meters.

The trail begins on the south side of the pass and is signed "RIFUGIO PISCIADU." The first 100 meters are spent climbing a grassy knoll and then the trail begins a gradual descent toward Corvara. At 1 km is a junction. The uphill trail climbs a steep, rocky gully to the Rifugio Pisciadu, crossing snow slopes and climbing a cliff with the aid of iron steps, cables, and, if you have them, carabiners. Although this trail is used by hundreds of hikers every day, it crosses a potentially dangerous snow slope and is beyond the scope of a hiking guide. So, unless you are a climber, stay on the lower trail.

Continue downhill and cross a gully. The way is poorly marked. Don't be confused by a trail coming up from the valley floor, or by the well-used trail heading for the waterfall. The route to Corvara continues down on an unmarked and rather obscure trail. (Before going farther, you might walk over to the waterfall and look up at the trail that climbs to Rifugio Pisciadu. It is impressive.) Your trail crosses under the falls and ½ km beyond passes a junction to Colfosco. Continue on to the next junction, which occurs shortly after crossing a rambunctious little creek. This junction is poorly signed but the way is obvious. Head down! The trail is rough and the ground loose, so take your time. Once on the valley floor, follow Trail 65, passing below the campground, then on to Corvara.

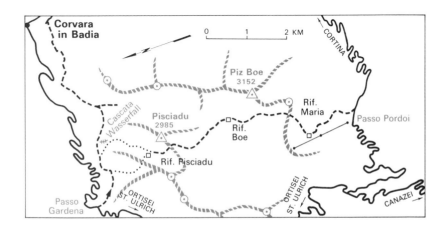

Hikers on the cable trail to Rifugio Pisciadu

The best way to explore the Sella Group of the Dolomites is to go by lift or trail from the Passo Pordoi to the Rifugio Maria and, from there, to follow Trails 627 and 666 past several other refuges to the Rifugio Pisciadu, located on the gigantic cliffs of the ranges' northern edge. If you are used to heights and have climbing skills, this is a highly recommended trip. Be sure to carry an ice axe, helmet, seat harness, slings, and carabiners.

94   PUEZ DOLOMITES

One way 11 km, 7 miles   **Elevation gain 390 meters,**
Hiking time 5 hours   **1279 feet**
High point 2528 meters, 8294 feet   **Map: Kompaß Wanderkarte 59**

Compared to the many breathtaking areas in the Dolomites, the Puez
Group might be considered of secondary interest. However, if rated in
terms of hikability, this area is top-notch. Once you are past the border
peaks, you enter a broad plateau, with meadows and white limestone
outcropping formed as either horizontal weathered sheets or low-lying
vertical ribs. Close inspection of the stone shows it is full of fossils. There
are several small lakes, high rounded hills, rock caps, and a canyonlike
valley called the Vallelunga, which cuts the plateau. Many well-marked
trails provide ample sport for the ambitious, adventurous wanderer. Several small huts offer sleeping space.

From the city of Corvara, take the bus to Passo Gardena, elevation
2137 meters. The trailhead is opposite the Rifugio Alpino. Head north on
Trail 2, marked "RIFUGIO PUEZ." The trail begins as a dirt road heading
toward Rifugio Cir and a chairlift. Walk along the road for a short distance. After a switchback, follow a trail to the right, across green pastureland, to more buildings and another chairlift where the trail forks
bewilderingly. Take the upper trail on the right marked Trail 2 to
"RIFUGIO PUEZ."

At 1 km, the trail winds around a small basin filled with fantastic rock
pillars. A quick side trip to the left is worth the extra time because of the
excellent views it offers. The trail arrives at Passo Cir, 2466 meters, with
views of the snowcapped Sella Group. A bit farther on, at the 2528-meter
Passo Crespeina, are views across the plateaulike midsection of the Puez
Group. Below the pass is Lago Crespeina. The trail passes the lake and
then crosses the rolling plateau to another pass, the Forcella Ciampai,

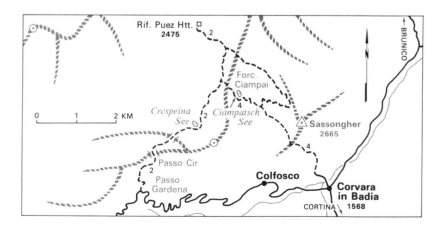

Hikers in the Puez Dolomites above Passo Gardena

2388 meters, at 4½ km. The pass lies at the head of two deep valleys. Trail 4, which is the best and the easiest route back to Corvara, begins here. Trail 4 passes a small lake called the Ciampatsch See and ends on a paved road in a group of houses above the city.

If you choose to continue to the Rifugio Puez, stay on Trail 2, crossing yet another pass. After walking 6½ km, arrive at a hut, which in itself is unimpressive. However, it is a useful place to stay and a good place from which to branch out and explore other trails.

Farmers' huts in meadows below the Hochhorn

95   HOCHHORN

Loop trip 16 km, 10 miles
Hiking time 7 hours
High point 2623 meters, 8606 feet

Elevation gain 1336 meters,
4383 feet
Map: Kompaß Wanderkarte 57

Standing on a high ridge, with one foot in Italy and one foot in Austria, you'll find magnificent views of both countries. The mountains along this section of the border are rolling and grass-covered, at odds with the needlelike summits of the Sextener Dolomites to the south and the equally impressive snow- and glacier-covered Hohe Tauern to the north.

This hike, a loop over the Hochhorn (sometimes written as Hochorn), can be completed in one day. However, the high ridgetops beckon and it would be easy to roam to the east and to the west of the Hochhorn for several days. Where to overnight is the problem. There are no huts, and campsites are limited. By midsummer water is not available at the higher elevations, so you may have to hunt around to find a place to pitch your tent.

The hike begins from the small town of St. Martin, which may be reached by bus from Monguelfo (Welsburg). If driving, head west from Toblach on Highway 100 for 10 km to Monguelfo and then go north up the Valle di Casies for 12.7 km. Drive into St. Martin and park in the town square, elevation 1287 meters.

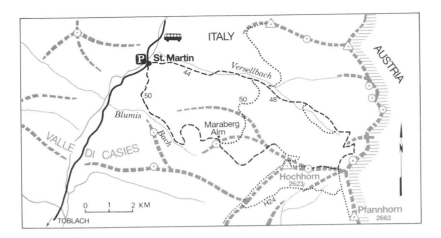

Walk up through town, passing the church on the right, to a large sign that marks the start of Trail 44. Pass a farm and then head up a steep hill on a gated dirt road. The road parallels the Versellbach up a narrow canyon and, after 2½ km, passes the first of many small shepherds' huts. At 3½ km one of the several Trail 50 spurs branches off to the right. Shortly after, Trail 48 heads off to the left, and a little beyond, Trail 44 divides. Take your pick—the two branches of Trail 44 rejoin at 2056 meters near the top of the pastureland. A wide trail continues the steep climb to a high ridge crest and the Italian–Austrian border, which is reached at 7½ km.

Head to the right along the ridge for ½ km to an intersection. Go right again on Trail H24. If time allows, the ridge-crest trail continues over to the Pfannhorn, the highest summit in the area. Trail H24 heads west, descending, climbing, and then descending as it rounds the Hochhorn. On the west side of the peak, the trail divides; go right and follow the ridge crest back to the east to reach the cross that marks the 2623-meter summit of Hochhorn at 9 km.

Now begins the tricky section of the loop, which should not be attempted in poor visibility. The loop follows Trail 50 off the summit to the northwest. There is no visible path, so navigate by following the painted rocks down the scree-covered slope to a 2510-meter saddle, and then go left and descend to the basin below. Head straight across the basin to find faint signs of the trail and follow it down to the farms and fields of Maraberg Alm, where the trail becomes a road.

When the road divides, go straight and cross a creek. In 100 meters the road divides again. Go left, past the farmhouses, and follow the road as it plummets down the narrow Blumis Bach valley.

Near the floor of the Valle di Casies, the road divides. Go right and descend to a fence. Head to the right, following the fence line around to a village street, and then descend to the start at the St. Martin town square.

96   TRE CIME

Round trip from Auronzo Hütte
11 km, 7 miles
Hiking time 5 hours
High point 2522 meters, 8272 feet

Elevation gain 700 meters,
2296 feet
Map: Kompaß Wanderkarte 58

Lakes and strangely eroded limestone pillars create an exotic setting for hikes in the Sextener Dolomiten. The objective of this hike is the Rifugio Locatelli, an extremely popular hut that can provide a base camp for further explorations.

The Rifugio Locatelli can be reached from the north, south, or west. From the south, travel by bus or car 14 km south from Toblach and then head east on "48 BIS" to Lake Misurina, where bus service ends. At the north end of the lake, turn east and drive up the steep road to Auronzo Hütte. Two km up the road is a tollbooth. Here, either pay the very expensive toll or park and walk the road to the hut. (The alternative to the long road walk is a scenic trail over the cliffs. Unfortunately, this trail should not be attempted until late summer when the steep and icy snow patches are melted.)

If you drove, park the car at 2320 meters and walk the service road, Trail 161, slightly downhill, under the towering walls of the Tre Cime for 2 km to Rifugio Lavaredo, 2390 meters. From the hut, follow Trail 101 over the Forcella di Lavaredo (Paternsattel), and then drop to the Rifugio Locatelli at 2438 meters, 3½ km. The four-storied hut stares out at the spires of Monte Paterno and the three summits of Tre Cime.

The hut is an excellent base for several days of excursions. If possible, however, avoid the hut in August when it is overcrowded with a worldwide assortment of hikers and climbers.

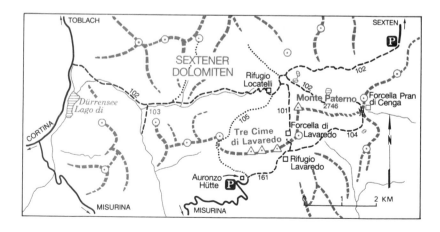

Chapel near Rifugio Locatelli

For the return, loop back on Trail 101, passing two lakes that lie below the hut, and then climb the 2522-meter Forcella Pran di Cenga. Remnants of the fierce fighting of World War I—caves, old gun emplacements, barbed wire, and rotting buildings—serve as a grim memorial in this beautiful place. The loop is completed on Trail 104, which leads back to Rifugio Lavaredo and then down the service road to the parking lot.

From the north, bus service is available to Sexten (Sesto). From there you must catch a taxi up the Fiscalina Valley to the trailhead and then climb for 6 km on Trail 105 to the hut.

From the west, the route follows the popular Trail 102 up the Valle de Rienza for 8 km to reach the Rifugio Locatelli. The hike begins from Highway 51 at 11 km south of the intersection with Highway 49 at Toblach. No camping is allowed in this area, so plan to stay at the hut.

SLOVENIA

The only portion of the former Yugoslavia covered in this book is the Julian Alps, a beautiful limestone massif in the Republic of Slovenia. Up to the end of World War I, this region was also part of Austria. The language, however, is Slovenian, which has absolutely no relationship to German, although many of the inhabitants can speak German. The people are very friendly and helpful to visitors. One note of caution: This was a communist country for many years and laws are strictly enforced. If camping, stay in a campground, and in the mountains, plan to overnight at a *dom* (hut). Expect to pay high prices for gas, food, camping, or lodging.

As in Italy, the mountain roads are very narrow and difficult to drive. Public transportation into the mountains is not as well organized here as in other parts of Europe. If you are relying on trains and buses, you may find yourself walking up some of the long, lonely valleys that approach the mountains. This can be a great adventure in itself, as Slovenia has retained much of the traditional atmosphere that has disappeared in the more prosperous areas of the Alps.

The northern Julian Alps (Hike No. 98) are very rugged and, as the Slovenian maps do not differentiate between trails for hikers and trails for climbers, a hike can easily turn into a rock-climbing adventure. If you have some climbing experience, bring your harness, slings, and carabiners and take advantage of the cables provided on these secured climbing routes. If you do not have climbing experience, be ready to turn back if the going gets tough, before you get into difficulties.

The best hiking is found in the southern Julian Alps (Hike Nos. 97, 99, and 100) where the terrain is rounded. Here trails ramble over rolling plains, past lakes and waterfalls to excellent vantage points of the rugged peaks to the north.

Note: In 1991 a very bloody civil war broke out in parts of the former Yugoslavia. At the time of this printing, the U.S. State Department considers the Republic of Slovenia itself to be safe for American travelers; however, before planning a trip to this region, check with the State Department's Travel Advisory Hotline. The number is 202-647-5225. Current information may be obtained while in Europe by inquiring at any U.S. embassies or consulates.

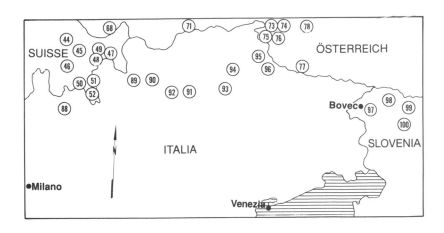

The Krma Valley (Hike No. 98)

97   LEPA KOMNA

Round trip to Krnsko Jezero
  8 km, 5 miles
Hiking time 3½ hours
High point 1463 meters, 4799 feet
Elevation gain 800 meters,
  2624 feet

Round trip to Dom Planina na
  Krau 21 km, 13 miles
Hiking time 2 days
High point 1803 meters, 5914 feet
Elevation gain 1500 meters,
  4920 feet
Maps: Julian Alps, East and West

The Lepa Komna, in the southern section of the Julian Alps, offers a great contrast to the rugged peaks that surround Mount Triglav (Hike No. 98). With rich meadows and low, rounded summits, this is ideal country for roaming. The whole area is crisscrossed with wagon roads built during World War I and long since overgrown. Still discernible, the roads pass abandoned barracks, old barbed-wire fences, and other relics of this tragic period of history.

From Bovec, drive north 1.5 km and then go left toward Krunjska Gora for 7.5 km. Find a road on the right marked "DOM DR. KLEMENTA JUGA." At 6 km the road ends at the hotel-restaurant, elevation 680 meters.

The trail begins from the parking lot, to the right of the hotel, and is signed "KRN-GOMISCKOVO ZAUE TISCE NA KRNU" 4½ hours, "KRNSKIH JEZERIN" 2 hours, and "DOM NA KOMNI" 4½ hours. The trail climbs steeply, rising 800 meters in 2 km, partly on wide military wagon roads. At 3½ km pass a farm and reach a trail junction. Regardless of your final destination, take the right-hand trail for ½ km to Krnsko Jezero, a lovely lake with no outlet, at 1383 meters. For day hikers, this is a natural turnaround point.

To reach Dom Planina na Krau, return to the junction and turn east, climbing first to a pass and then heading across a large green meadow.

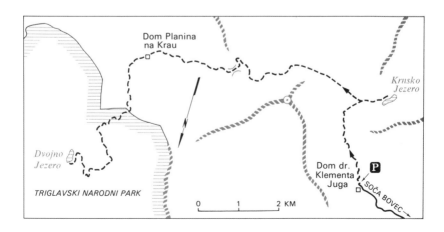

At 5 km pass the roofless remnants of a huge barracks and many other small buildings. The trail continues, with more ups than downs, crossing over a 1803-meter pass at 7 km from the end of the road.

From the pass, the trail drops 300 meters in the next 3½ km to the Dom Planina na Krau, a hut located at the edge of the forest at 1513 meters, 10½ km from the road. Several days may be spent here, taking loop hikes into Triglavski Park and scrambling up some of the nearby peaks.

Krnsko Jezero

98   MOUNT TRIGLAV (DOM STANIČA)

Round trip 20 km, 12½ miles
Hiking time two days
High point 2332 meters, 7649 feet

Elevation gain 1420 meters,
   4658 feet
Map: Julian Alps, East

This hike runs along the flanks of the highest peak in Slovenia, the 2863-meter Mount Triglav, to a high mountain hut, Dom Staniča. From the hut, several days may be spent exploring the large network of trails. Be careful though: Some trails traverse or climb sheer cliffs and these dangers are not indicated on the maps. If exploring, ask for route information before starting out and carry a climbing harness, slings, and carabiners to hook on to the cables. Since the Julian Alps are formed from limestone, water generally runs below the surface and is not accessible to a thirsty hiker, so carry a liter or two on every hike. Note: You *must* stay in the huts. This is a national park and no camping is allowed.

Two well-marked trails lead to Dom Staniča. If you have rock-climbing proclivities and the proper gear, the trail from Aljažev Dom is fun and exciting. This steep trail quickly turns into a climbing route as it makes its way up the cliffs with the aid of an occasional iron spike handhold, a cable handrail to negotiate a hair-raising ledge, and a 100-meter cable securing the route up a sheer rock wall.

For an easier assault, try the Krma Valley, on an excellent trail. For either approach, drive to the town of Mojstrana, located between the Italian border and Jesenice. The town is off the main highway, so watch carefully for the well-signed turnoff. The road winds up through town and then divides. For the Aljažev Dom Trail, go right, to the end of the Vrata Valley. To reach the Krma Valley, stay left on the road to Jesenice for 100 meters. Turn right, following the sign to Krma on a strange little

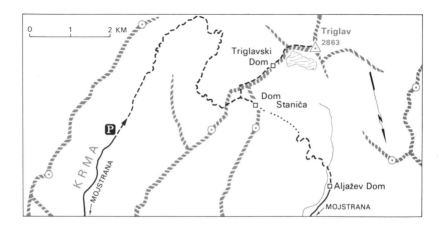

The Krma Valley, Tosc (mountain) in center

road that climbs steeply, is very narrow, and has no turnouts. After 200 meters the road divides yet again; go straight uphill on pavement, then dirt, and then pavement again. At 3.3 km is an intersection. Stay right, still following the "KRMA" signs. At 4.8 km from Mojstrana, after driving through a farm, there is an unmarked intersection. Go right. At 9 km pass a hotel and at 12½ km the road ends, elevation 910 meters.

The trail, used by pack horses to supply the various huts, heads up the valley and is marked with a red circle and a white dot. The way gradually steepens as it climbs through forest to a junction. Keep right and head up through rock-strewn meadows to reach several forest huts and two more junctions. Keep right again, staying on the horse trail. At 2017 meters, 7 km from the end of the road, the terrain changes: vegetation becomes sparse and rocks are strangely eroded. The grade lessens as the trail nears a 2250-meter pass at 9 km. A bit farther, there is another junction. The left-hand trail follows a ridge to Triglavski Dom and continues up to the summit of Mount Triglav. Take the right-hand trail to reach Dom Staniča at 2332 meters. Although the hike to the *dom* only takes about 5 hours, most people are ready to call it a day.

99   LAKE BLED

Loop trip 3½ km, 2¼ miles
Hiking time 1½ hours
High point 685 meters, 2247 feet

Elevation gain 260 meters, 853 feet
Map: Julian Alps, East, or the free
   tourist map

The glacial Blejsko Jezero (Lake Bled), with a baroque church on its small island, is the most photogenic spot in the Slovenian Alps. With a rich, thousand-year-old history, the lake and city of Bled have recently become favorite retreats for heads of state and hordes of tourists. But the popularity of Lake Bled has not destroyed its subtle beauty.

The resort city of Bled, in the eastern section of the Julian Alps of Slovenia, is reached by car, bus, or train. The best view of this area, and the objective of this hike, is from a high hill at the southwest end of the lake, near the campground. The trail is easy to locate. Simply follow the main road through the city and around the lake. There is a wide walking path around the lake but no bus service. Parking at the trailhead is very limited and you must find an available spot along the lakeshore or near the campground.

The trailhead is located 500 meters south of the campground. The trail sign notes three destinations, including "OSOJNICA 6," elevation 495 meters. Just to the south of this trailhead, note the steps coming down the hill—the return portion of the loop.

The trail heads right, up into the forest on an old road. Each time you reach an intersection, follow the path marked with the number 6. About halfway up the hill, the trail divides. On the right, a spur trail makes a short, steep ascent to the top of a rocky knoll and the first viewpoint. Enjoy the view and then head on; the best is still ahead.

Back at the intersection, go left and continue the climb to the crest of a rib, where the trail divides again. The trail on the right follows the rib for another kilometer to the forested summit of Mount Osojnica, a 756-

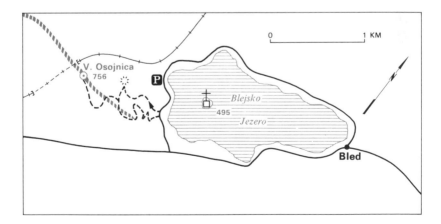

Lake Bled from Osojnia Trail

meter-high hill. Unfortunately, the view from the summit is limited, although in mid-July the many wild cyclamen blooming on the forest floor make this a delightful extension to the hike. To reach the viewpoints, go left from the intersection. Follow the rib line, arrows, and the number 6 to three overlooks. The first overlooks the Sava Bohinjka valley. The next two viewpoints overlook Lake Bled.

From the third viewpoint, the trail descends an iron stairway and then heads down a well-graded trail to the lakeshore.

100 TRIGLAVSKI NARODNI PARK—SOUTH

Loop trip 19 km, 12 miles
Hiking time 7 hours
High point 1700 meters, 5577 feet

Elevation gain 1040 meters,
3412 feet
Map: Julian Alps, East

While the northern end of Triglavski Narodni Park (Mount Triglav National Park) is mainly for mountain climbers, the southern end of the park has endless opportunities for one-day or extended hikes. The terrain has a strange aspect to it. It is eroded as only limestone can be: steep gullies, weird rock formations, and odd depressions. Caves and sinkholes are common. Most streams flow underground, emerging as thundering rivers and waterfalls in the valleys below.

To reach the southern end of the park, turn off the main highway south of Jesenice and drive through Bled. Head southwest around Lake Bled to a major intersection and follow the signs south for 18.3 km to the town of Boh. Bistrica. Turn right and drive another 6.2 km west to Bohinjsko Jezero. At the lake, stay left and follow the signs 9.5 km to the end of the road at Dom Savica, elevation 660 meters. If you are relying on public transportation, the train goes as far as Relisting Bistrica. Beyond there you must catch the local bus to the end of the road.

From Dom Savica, the first task is to hike up the steep walls that box in the end of the valley. There are two options: the trail up the north wall of the valley, called the Relinking, or the trail on the west side to Dom na Komni. The Relinking Trail is a real cliff-hanger: very steep, with an occasional cable for security. But it is an excellent trail, if you have a good head for heights. The Dom na Komni Trail follows a World War I wagon

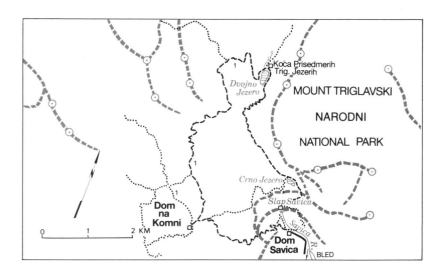

Dom na Komni

road out of the valley. This trail is wide and well graded with endless switchbacks.

To hike the loop, it is suggested to go up the Relinking Trail and descend via Dom na Komni. In between, the loop passes Črno Jezero, a small forested lake surrounded by cliffs, at 1340 meters, and then heads upvalley to the Koča Prisedmerih Trig. Jezerih, a hut situated on a pretty lake at 1683 meters. At this point the loop joins Trail 1 (also referred to as 7J). Head southwest on Trail 1 to Dom na Komni and then descend. Views along the entire loop are excellent, with mountains visible in all directions.

To truly enjoy this area, it is best to spend several days taking side trips and exploring. If staying in a hut, aim for the Dom na Komni, which has its own supply lift and is almost always open. Remember, no camping is allowed within the national park.

Names and Addresses of Alpine Clubs
(Main Branches)

France	Club Alpin Français 9, rue de la Boetie, 75008 Paris
Italy	Club Alpine Italiano, via Ugo Foscole 3 20121 Milano
Switzerland	Geschaftsstelle SAC, Helvetiaplatz 4 3005 Bern
Liechtenstein	Liechtensteiner Alpenverein, F1-9490 Vaduz
Germany	Deutscher Alpenverein Praterinsel 5, 8 Munich 22
Austria	Osterreichischer Alpenverein Wilhelm-Greil-Strasse 15, 6010 Innsbruck

Names and Addresses of
Trail-Managing Organizations

Fédération Française de la Randonnée Pedestre
64 rue de Gergovie
75014 Paris
Phone: 47 23 62 32

Comité National des Sentiers de Grande Randonnée
8, avenue Marceau
75008 Paris

Schweizer Arbeitsgemeinschaft für Wanderwege
Im Hirshalm 49
4125 Riehen/Switzerland
Phone: (031) 54 91 11

INDEX

About the Authors

Photographer and writer VICKY SPRING is the author of *Bicycling the Pacific Coast* and *Cross Country Ski Tours in Washington 1 & 2*, and co-author of *Hiking the Great Northwest* (The Mountaineers). She resides near Seattle, Washington.

Between hiking and cross-country skiing trips, author and filmmaker HARVEY EDWARDS has written six books and many articles for travel, business, and skiing magazines, and has produced and directed more than twenty documentary films. A former twenty-year resident of Chamonix, France, he now lives in Eagle Bridge, New York.

THE MOUNTAINEERS, founded in 1906, is a non-profit outdoor activity and conservation club, whose mission is "to explore, study, preserve and enjoy the natural beauty of the outdoors...." Based in Seattle, Washington, the club is now the third largest such organization in the United States, with 12,000 members and four branches throughout Washington State.

The Mountaineers sponsors both classes and year-round outdoor activities in the Pacific Northwest, which include hiking, mountain climbing, ski-touring, snowshoeing, bicycling, camping, kayaking and canoeing, nature study, sailing, and adventure travel. The club's conservation division supports environmental causes through educational activities, sponsoring legislation, and presenting informational programs. All club activities are led by skilled, experienced volunteers, who are dedicated to promoting safe and responsible enjoyment and preservation of the outdoors.

The Mountaineers Books, an active, non-profit publishing program of the club, produces guidebooks, instructional texts, historical works, natural history guides, and works on environmental conservation. All books produced by The Mountaineers are aimed at fulfilling the club's mission.

If you would like to participate in these organized outdoor activities or the club's programs, consider a membership in The Mountaineers. For information and an application, write or call The Mountaineers, Club Headquarters, 300 Third Avenue West, Seattle, Washington 98119; (206) 284-6310.